SYMPHONY

THE ART OF MANAGING CHANGE

TRICIA BENNETT

Copyright © 2022 Tricia Bennett

All rights reserved. No part of this book may be reproduced in any form or by any electronic or mechanical means, including information storage and retrieval systems, without written permission from the author, except in the case of a reviewer, who may quote brief passages embodied in critical articles or in a review.

Trademarked names are used in an editorial fashion, with no intention of infringement of the respective owner's trademark.

The information contained in this book is for general information and entertainment purposes only. The recommendations, opinions, experiences, observations, or other information contained herein is provided "as is" and neither the author nor publisher make any representations or warranties of any kind, express or implied, about the accuracy, suitability, reliability, or completeness of this book's content. Any reliance a reader places on such information is therefore strictly at their own risk. All recommendations are made without guarantee on the part of the author and publisher. To the maximum extent permitted by law, the author and publisher disclaim all liability from this publication's use. In no event will either author or publisher be liable to any reader for any loss or damage whatsoever arising from the use of the information contained in this book. This book is not a substitute for professional services and readers are advised to seek professional guidance when required.

Printed in the United States of America
First Printing, 2022
BDOT Enterprises, LLC

TheSymphonyMethod.com

Cover design, interior layout, and illustrations by Victoria Wolf of Wolf Design and Marketing

Author photograph by Stephen Russell

Editing and Publishing Services provided by Positively Powered Publications

978-0-578-35609-9

To My Mom (Kay), Sandi, Vera, Marilyn, and all other foremothers who endured much to pave the way so that the women of my generation and of those that follow have more freedom and more choices.

To Chris, Kacey and Katy, for your constant love and encouragement, and for being both my most honest critics and my biggest fans.

To Emily and Tom, for whom I envision a healthier, peaceful, more inclusive world. May you experience bliss often and experience the achievement of Symphony many times over.

CONTENTS

Prologue vii

PART I: LAYING THE GROUNDWORK—MANAGING PERFORMANCE

Chapter 1: What is Change Management? 1

Chapter 2: It Starts with One. Managing the
Performance of a Single Individual 11

Chapter 3: One to Many—Proactively Planning
Performance for the Organization 61

PART II: GETTING TACTICAL—LET'S DO THIS!

Chapter 4: The Change Management Wheel 71

Chapter 5: The Starting Point—Defining the Vision 83

Chapter 6: Anticipating Motivating Factors 103

Chapter 7: Aligning Process and Technology 121

Chapter 8: Building Capability 139

Chapter 9: Accountability and Recognition 167

Chapter 10: Iterate and Improve 189

Chapter 11: Imagine the Possibilities 205

Appendix Process and Tools 215

Pioneers of Professional Development,
Process Improvement, and Change Management 235

Acknowledgments 243

About the Author 245

PROLOGUE

I STARTED WRITING THIS BOOK on June 4, 2020. Today we are in the midst of a global pandemic, and our freedom to move around our cities is just starting to open up again. Organizations everywhere have been thrown into rapidly changing conditions and have had no choice but to respond. Wherever possible, employers are transitioning from on-premise work to work-from-home environments. Employees, as humans do, are adapting as best as they can and wondering what the future holds. People are looking for leadership, and true leaders are emerging. Organizations have an unprecedented opportunity to demonstrate their own leadership and show what their corporate cultures are made of.

In the midst of this pandemic, we're finding that Black and Brown communities are being hit harder by the virus itself—most certainly by limited access to the best living conditions, healthiest food, and best healthcare. The socioeconomic challenges that surround the virus, such as the inability to perform work from home and the challenges related to closed schools, are hitting minority communities the hardest. These facts make it apparent that while our nation has made some progress since the civil rights movement in the 1960s, there is still far too much to be done.

To make this reality even worse, a Minneapolis police officer killed a forty-six-year-old member of one of the largely Black communities in North Minneapolis, George Floyd, by pressing his knee into the victim's neck for almost nine minutes. Despite Mr. Floyd's repeated protests that he couldn't breathe, the police officer continued his restraint for a full three minutes after Mr. Floyd became motionless. From our quarantine bubbles, we watched as people reacted—we saw shock, angry protests, violence, destruction, and looting. We saw law enforcement and troops of the national guard use tear gas and rubber bullets to disperse angry crowds—and we saw multi-racial peaceful protests, tearful hugs, flowers, and people trying to figure out how to help. We asked ourselves, "What, really, can we do to help?" Again, leaders emerged, and organizations spoke out to their people.

Our organizations, the groups, projects, and teams we lead are made up of people, and each individual is responding and reacting to these situations in very different ways. The way we respond as leaders shapes the cultures of the organizations we work in and articulates what we stand for. The choices we make as we implement new ways of working matter. Our ability to anticipate what our organizations need, and our intentional implementation of processes and policies require thoughtful leadership, empathy, and open, authentic communication.

There is a need for the proactive management of change now more than ever, and an opportunity for leaders to demonstrate what their organizations stand for. Over the years, many have asked me to help them understand how they can effectively

PROLOGUE

manage change. I'm writing this book to provide some insight into how leaders can successfully work with their groups during these uncertain times and when we emerge from them.

I have been helping organizations manage some elements of change for almost thirty years. Through these years of work, my teams, colleagues, fellow leaders, and I have also been able to leave some of our own values behind in the companies and communities we have touched. I have had the amazing opportunity to observe and experience so many organizational cultures that I have lost count. My work has been primarily around supporting change as we implement new technology, but with every change effort, we experience and influence culture too.

As leaders, we establish the vision for our organizations, whether we mean to or not. We can choose to do so intentionally. We can choose to empathize and anticipate. We can choose to include rather than exclude. We can choose to be authentic and transparent in our communication. We can choose to model and expect high standards. We can challenge ourselves to inspire others. And we can intentionally craft the cultures of the organizations and teams we work with. Most importantly, we can care about the experiences our people have, the cultures we're creating and approach this leadership work in a service-minded way.

All of the leadership concepts I've listed above are elements of change management. In writing this, I'm hoping to connect some concepts, offer some new perspectives, and provide a few tools and examples that help leaders to manage the change in their organizations with intention. I have a habit of reading business books on the subjects of sales, leadership, professional development, and change. With each read, I take away a nugget or two that

SYMPHONY

become part of my professional fabric. I hope you find a nugget or two here.

I call this book *Symphony* because the art of managing organizational change is like conducting a symphony. If you ever watch an orchestra conductor and the players in the string section and the woodwinds and the brass and the percussion all working together—it's an excellent visual metaphor for what we're trying to achieve in high-performing teams, organizations, and even communities. An orchestra represents a group of individual contributors, with some interspersed leaders, who all know what they're supposed to do, and why they're supposed to do it. They're practiced in their abilities and are growing all the time. They're motivated to play well, and the conductor helps to set the vision and sway the collective energy. The conductor provides perspective to keep the group focused on the desired outcome. Not one of them can achieve the desired outcome as an individual, but when these individual contributors come together as a part of a group, the result can be *magical*.

When you become practiced in managing change, and you collectively achieve your results a time or two, you and the other individual contributors who make up your orchestra will do masterful work and feel proud and accomplished about being a part of something great. Your group, community, or organization as a whole will improve because this type of excellent team has the ability to deliver even greater outcomes than you may have been able to imagine.

Part I:

LAYING THE GROUNDWORK— MANAGING PERFORMANCE

Chapter 1:

WHAT IS CHANGE MANAGEMENT?

LET'S CONSIDER HOW MUCH CHANGE our entire globe went through during the first half of 2020. One day, we all were told that businesses were going to close and we had to stay at home. We didn't have the opportunity to plan proactively, so we did the best we could. Some countries, states, and communities had better plans and leaders in place than others, and had better outcomes than others. But we were all motivated in some way—most by doing our parts to minimize the spread of the pandemic, some because we had no other choice—so we changed.

As we look back and explore the leaders who emerged, they were people we felt were communicating authentically and factually. They were people who didn't just tell us what we wanted to hear—they told us the good, the bad, and the ugly. These leaders told it like it was, connected with us as individuals, and gained our trust. They didn't need us to like them. They just cared enough about us to tell us what was happening, explained the reasons behind their decisions, and asked us for our cooperation.

In the businesses, organizations, and projects we lead, we're fortunate. We typically know what changes we want to make before we make them, so we have an opportunity to proactively manage and take a structured approach to communication, training, support, measurement, and recognition. We can lead proactively and respectfully. This isn't a huge level of effort. It is a routine approach we can adopt. In fact, it is so simple to do it seems like common sense! This proactive and intentional approach to helping our teams and organizations move from point A to point B is what we refer to as change management.

Still, every day, organizations embark on initiatives without a defined approach or even an intention for managing the change people will experience. When this occurs, often the desired outcomes fall short, or there are delays in realizing the benefits. Sometimes, poor management of change can result in unnecessary emotional reactions by those who are expected to adopt it. This often creates a negative impact on culture and chips away at the credibility of a team and its leadership.

Today, in addition to all of the other changes that organizations face, our businesses and communities are adjusting to new norms of working remotely and managing public health. They have a renewed awareness of racial tensions in our communities and have been presented with a reality check about how well they're doing with diversity and inclusion. We have become painfully aware of deeply divided loyalties to political parties. We've learned about our organizations from these national and globe-altering experiences. Those insights present a *huge opportunity* for organizational leaders to build trust and credibility and adopt new ways of working that involve visionary leadership, effective and transparent communication, and inclusion. This is a time when companies and communities can discuss their cultures, openly discuss challenges, articulate what they stand for, inspire their team and community members, and build understanding and loyalty. This is an excellent time to adopt and apply change management principles to lead and build culture.

DEFINITIONS

If you look up the words "change management," you'll find several definitions that range from simple dictionary definitions to extensive Wikipedia references. Many reputable organizations that teach change management and offer services have great definitions too. Some IT organizations have a different definition of change management that refers to a process used to manage code or application changes. I tend to refer to this as IT changing governance to prevent the confusion of terms. For the purpose of this book, I'll stick with mine:

> **Change Management:** *Employing a proactive, structured approach to guide a group of people from engaging in one behavior, set of behaviors or mindset to engaging in a different behavior, set of behaviors or mindset so that it achieves an objective or desired outcome.*

Simply put, our organization has an objective or desired outcome, and we're using a structured, planned approach to help our people move from point A to point B.

It is important to note that change is likely to happen anyway, even if it is not managed using a structured, proactive approach. Sometimes it happens sporadically, sometimes it happens poorly, sometimes it happens with unnecessary frustration, and sometimes it happens without fully achieving the desired outcomes. Conversely, sometimes the change (or at least part of it) makes so much sense that it is well adopted with minimal proactive effort.

Commitment to the intentional management of the changes occurring in an organization becomes part of its personality and sets the standard for the rapport leaders have with the teams they serve. An organization's personality, its standards of engagement, the authenticity in its communication, and how much it cares about the experience of its team members are the things that make up its culture. I believe we have a responsibility as leaders to not only achieve our business objectives, but to craft our organizational cultures. These cultures represent the energy we marinate in every single day. These cultures say who we are and what we represent. They help us attract and retain the best talent. They help us to uphold the highest standards of work. And they help us serve our communities and our globe.

WHY MANAGE CHANGE?

Other than the intrinsic desire we may have to be good leaders and establish good cultures, why else might we want to manage change? How about these ideas:

The workforce is changing, and the skilled workers you want to have on your teams expect much from their organizations. The talented and reliable workers that you want are shopping for the right employer just as much as you are shopping for the right team members. Team members want to align with a vision, want to be inspired by leadership, want to be recognized, want to feel included and valued, and want to do work that matters. The way you manage the changes going on in your organization is the way you develop rapport with the people you lead. Some of your most loyal, skilled, and mature employees are retiring and even with the pandemic unemployment, your new, highly skilled talent will have a choice of employers.

By 2025 some sources project that as many as 75% of workers will be of the millennial generation or younger. Will your team represent the A team? Will your team be the place where people feel valued and inspired to do high-quality work?

On the financial side of things, change management is a no-brainer. I've worked on technology implementations for years. I marvel at how relatively simple it is to gain financial approval for resources allocated to the technical elements of the project like architecture, development, and licensing. It's much easier than gaining financial approval for resources allocated to the people elements of the project, like communication, training, recognition, accountability and generating real engagement. In the end, if your people don't adopt the change, what is the point of implementing the solution in the first place?

I've seen plenty of leaders of organizations choose not to invest in managing the change or choose not to follow through on the efforts they planned. These organizations often experience slow adoption and dwindling ROI. Conversely, I've seen leaders invest in change management, who saw adoption of the desired change reach engagement, who experienced ROI that occurred faster than anticipated and in ways that they hadn't previously imagined.

In my opinion, if the stakes are high, the investments are high, or the ROI expectations are high, taking a proactive approach to aligning the behaviors, activities, and mindsets of the people who will be called on to adopt the change is a critical investment.

A STORY

Many years ago, I worked with an amazing organization that sold life sciences equipment and supplies to health care and educational institutions. They had a seasoned sales team that, when tallied, had an *average* length of employment of seventeen years. That's a long time! More than 1,200 people globally were going to undergo the change of moving from a spreadsheet-based sales tracker to using a full customer relationship management (CRM) and pipeline management tool. While these people were incredibly smart, few were excited about moving to a seemingly more complex, digital platform for managing their sales activity. What was unique about this organization, though, was the loyalty of the teams and the commitment by leaders to supporting their people.

The CIO decided to form a team of five people, who, for a full-time eighteen months, would become experts and communicate, care for, and provide a direct line of support for this team as they adopted the new technology. They would travel the globe more than once to bring personalized support to the various regions.

The CIO aligned with the sales leaders to communicate the vision. She invested in the training and planning and in the care team. She oversaw the important details as the project unfolded, and was very pleased as the adoption gained momentum and the team became engaged in their new technology. Many organizations have super users, champions, and teams of people who are given the responsibility of support in addition to their day jobs. But this service-focused mindset and commitment to ensuring the success of the implementation by this CIO stood out for me.

At one point, I was approached by one of the participants after attending an in-person training class. He had struggled through many of the exercises and knew he was going to need some extra care. He said, "Tricia, I just wanted to thank you and the care team for providing the training you did, and especially for providing these well-written instructions. Obviously, I struggle a bit with the computer part, but I am committed to helping the company do this. It makes such good sense! I'm probably going to retire in a couple of years, and I really don't know how I'll figure out how to use this program, but I'll ask my son to help me, and I know these work instructions are going to be really helpful to him."

This is an example of a culture that was as committed to its people as the people were to it. It was an amazing environment to be in, and the energy of the organization was positive and supportive. It's not uncommon for a person who struggles the most during class come up and share appreciation for the support and materials, but rarely do I have someone state that loyalty to the organization is the reason that he's going to figure it out. This guy had no intention of actually doing the work in the CRM system, but he was going to be sure the work got done because he was loyal to the organization and trusted the vision of his leaders. In the end, not only did this team achieve its initial objectives to have visibility into the sales pipeline and the ability to aggregate information for their customer base that would help them make well-informed decisions, but they surpassed their adoption goals and timelines and found ROI in even more ways than they initially anticipated.

Several years after the initial implementation, the CIO called me again to say that they had been involved in an acquisition. The company that had acquired them used different systems. She said that during the transition meetings, she and the sales leaders asked that the new leadership not require the sales team to change CRM solutions. Also, over the years the system had evolved, and they were getting so much out of it that they didn't want to interrupt the momentum they had gained. The CIO and the sales leaders got their wish, and I had the opportunity to work with them again as they on-boarded a new team.

It seems easy right? So why doesn't every organization do it?

Change management often just feels like common sense, and it does seem easy. Frank Lloyd Wright (and Voltaire) both remind us, however, "There is nothing more uncommon than common sense." Just because some might consider something to be easy to do doesn't mean it is going to get done.

Too often, organizations assume that they know what their people want and how they're going to respond. They assume that their people are going to have the bandwidth and the skill set to coordinate communication, training, and follow-up. They underestimate the time commitment and overestimate the simplicity of the task. Often, when we're immersed in the day-to-day challenges of getting the work done, some of the tasks that are considered easy fall through the cracks or get prioritized as less important than something else. In the end they just can fall into

WHAT IS CHANGE MANAGEMENT?

the category of missed opportunity.

The previous story provides an excellent example of the commitment to success by clearing away the day job duties for the care team. Organizations everywhere do a great job of managing change by simply incorporating the activities into their project plans, creating accountability for the oversight, or by hiring consulting resources to help them do the work. Still, many miss their opportunity to manage the change well.

Here are some of the reasons I've heard people provide for not employing a structured approach to change management.

- The change is so easy—our teams will figure it out
- The need for this is so obvious. Why wouldn't people want to make this change?
- I already know how our people are going to react. So, taking the time to do this process will just add time, scope, and budget to our project.
- The approved budget is entirely allocated to building the solution. Our managers will handle the communication and training.
- We're over budget—something has to go—we'll take on the training and communication internally.
- Change management is a "nice to have," but doesn't really contribute to the ROI, so therefore, it is expendable.
- It's their job! If they don't do it, they won't have one.

There's no doubt that some of these are legitimate reasons. Budgets always have their limits, and I think decisions are most often made with the best intentions. However, some of my reasons for writing this book are to elevate the importance of intentionally managing change and to enable managers of people and projects to incorporate some of these principles into their own professional toolboxes.

SOME MISCONCEPTIONS

Before we move on, I want to talk about some misconceptions about change management. Intentionally managing change is *not* about making sure that *everyone* is happy about the change, or that they even buy into it. It isn't about selling an idea to a group of people, and it's not a guarantee that everyone is going to successfully adopt the change. It isn't about taking a team approach to deciding if or how a change should be made, though incorporating team feedback is often a good idea.

The decisions we make in organizations are often not intended to be democratic ones. But intentionally managing change says that we both expect and honor that individuals have different responses to changes, and that, as leaders, we will communicate authentically and give each person the time and space to move through their reactions. The principles explored in this book detail an approach that respectfully communicates, acknowledges reactions, makes space for discussion, provides support, builds rapport, and maximizes adoption.

Chapter 2:

IT STARTS WITH ONE. MANAGING THE PERFORMANCE OF A SINGLE INDIVIDUAL

BEFORE WE TALK ABOUT HOW to intentionally manage change for a whole group of people, let's first examine why individual members of a group may or may not perform in the ways we want them to.

Organizations, like orchestras, are simply groupings of individuals, so we need to focus on why individual players do what they do first—before we can focus on the larger group. In organizations, we typically refer to this as performance management. There are a lot of different flavors of performance management, and I think you'll find that most have the components we'll explore in this chapter.

How is this relevant to managing change? Because managing change is simply applying a proactive approach to guiding *many* individuals to perform in a desired way. Organizations are made up of a whole bunch of individuals. If we can proactively anticipate why people might or might not change, and do our best to address all those reasons in advance, we have a recipe for success!

This recipe works for small teams, medium teams, and even huge teams because we simply anticipate why an individual contributor may or may not be prepared to perform in a way that we want them to, and proactively address those reasons to maximize ability, motivation, adoption and, thus, performance.

It also turns out that applying performance models proactively helps us to empathize, communicate effectively, proactively prepare, and more authentically interact with our teams. In essence, it helps us to do the things that organizations with excellent cultures do. Quite a bonus! We'll get back to managing individual performance in the next chapter, but first, let me introduce a few more nuggets of excellence that have informed this approach.

Before we move on any further, I must pay homage to two gentlemen, Robert Mager and Peter Pipe, who developed a performance analysis model a very long time ago. I've provided more detail about their books in the 'Pioneers of Professional Development, Process Improvement and Change Management' section of the appendix, but the performance diagnostic approach that I refer to in this chapter is largely based on the approach of these two people. Be sure to check out the appendix, you won't want to miss the brilliant contributions of these two gentlemen for guiding people to success.

So, what is the diagnostic approach? Do tell!

IT STARTS WITH ONE.

Very often, leaders jump to the assumption that people who don't perform don't do so because they simply don't know how. So we assume that if we just teach people again it will solve the problem, right? Hmmm...not always. The diagnostic approach that we're about to walk through explores the other possible reasons, too, and may help your organization use those training budget dollars even more effectively. At the very least, you'll understand the fundamental reasons behind why people do and don't perform, how we can proactively and positively manage performance, and how we can tweak this model just a bit and apply it to larger groups of people to promote the successful achievement of organizational or community objectives.

If, as a senior leader, manager, supervisor, program manager, instructor, or team leader, you find that someone is not performing in the desired way, you can ask yourself the following questions to figure out why:

1. Does the person know what they're supposed to be doing and why you want them to do it?
2. Does the technology and/or other processes you're asking this person to use align nicely with the new change?
3. Does this person know how to do what you're asking them to do?
4. Does anyone know if this person is performing in the desired way? Does anyone care?
5. Is this person being rewarded for poor performance or punished for adhering to the process or desired behavior?
6. Does this person have the inherent skill set necessary to perform the required task?

7. Is this person motivated to do what you're asking? Is there something in it for them? Does it align well with their core values?

This is a seven-step list for diagnosing non-performance, and we're going to explore each of these elements in greater detail eventually. (This list is informed by Mager and Pipe's work in *Analyzing Performance Problems*.) Notice that only one of these performance factors is actually related to training. If people know how but aren't performing in the desired way, then one of the other factors is the culprit.

DEFICIENCY QUESTION:	WHAT TO DO ABOUT IT:
1. Does this person know what they're supposed to be doing and why you want them to do it?	If no: Tell them what you want them to do and how it fits into the big picture.
2. Does the technology and/or other processes you're asking this person to use align nicely with the new change?	If no: Evaluate and remove barriers to align the processes and technology.
3. Does this person know how to do what you're asking them to do?	If no: Provide training and coaching support to ensure capability.

4.	Does anyone know if this person is performing in the desired way? Does anyone care?	If no: Remind the person of the desired performance and then ensure that systems of accountability are in place to lend transparency to successful performance.
5.	Is this person being rewarded for poor performance or punished for adhering to the process or desired behavior?	If yes: Change the rewards and consequences so they are appropriately aligned with desirable performance.
6.	Does this person have the inherent skill set necessary to perform the required task?	If no: Consider whether this person is well suited for the work you want them to do, or invest in them to help them gain the skill set.
7.	Is this person motivated to do what you're asking? Is there something in it for them? Does it align well with their core values?	If no: Explore and discuss the intrinsic and extrinsic motivating factors for this person. Acknowledge challenges and highlight benefits.

If you've exhausted this list and you still haven't figured out why this person isn't performing, try asking them why they're *not* performing. (You might be able to save yourself some time by starting with that question.)

Now that we've introduced the entire list, let's explore each element more and connect them with examples that will help make them real. You might be thinking, "Hey! What does all of this individual performance stuff have to do with managing change?" Hang in there! These very simple performance management concepts are at the foundation of managing change. Managing organizational change is simply the art of anticipating what will ensure the success of a group of individuals. If we anticipate the possible answers to each of these individual diagnostic questions and proactively prepare, we have just gained the recipe for managing the change for a whole group of people.

A SCENARIO

"Joe" works on an internal team that has been asked to report how they use their time to support project work. Joe has been submitting his time sheets late every month, and *you* are his manager trying to figure out why. This simple scenario helps us consider different perspectives and possibilities. Before we embark on this diagnostic journey, however, I feel I should explain my personal relationship with time entry.

A STORY

I really *hate* entering time. When I first did it, I was an hourly employee, and we used time clocks. It felt micromanaging to me. It also could be used against me. If I clocked in late, it could count as a *tardy* and if I clocked in too early, I was trying to *pad my time sheet*. I couldn't win! But I did it because that's what you do when you're an hourly employee, and I wanted to get paid. It felt like my employment, paycheck, and ability to feed my kid depended on it, so I was highly motivated to comply.

As a salaried or freelance consultant, while I still really didn't like doing time sheets, it was a way of thoroughly detailing the work on

IT STARTS WITH ONE.

a particular client's behalf and made justifying billable hours easy. In fact, only once in my career have I ever had a client question how I billed my time, and I had the detail to back it up. As a freelance consultant, my time entries meant how much I could invoice, and when I led a group of consultants, the time entries rolled up to our overall revenue. While the entries were often very detailed and painful to enter, at the end, it felt rewarding to see the revenue roll-up because choosing self-employment had been a pretty big step for me.

Another time, I was asked to do a time sheet because I worked for a centralized team in a company that had multiple business units. The time data was used to allocate and justify our salaries across the enterprise. At one point I worked on projects for five of the units, two of which had multiple projects. This was complex and tedious work, using a time-entry system that wasn't well designed for this level of complexity. Other members of my team had much simpler time entry and got their entries in on time. I always waited until the last minute to do it and was frequently late. I did it because my manager asked me to, and I was both loyal to her and appreciated the need for accounting. In the end, I talked to the person who rolled up the time entries and sent her a quick summary at the end of each month that took about fifteen minutes to prepare. It got the job done and gave her what she needed. Getting my time back felt like a reward, even though I ultimately bypassed the time-entry system entirely.

At different times during my career, I had different relationships with capturing time and submitting time sheets. If I, as an individual contributor, have been influenced in all these ways, think about the different ways people feel when they are asked to use a new time-entry system.

SYMPHONY

Now that you have a little background on my relationship with time entry and why I chose this scenario, let's get back to Joe. These scenarios further demonstrate how a performance conversation might unfold using the diagnostic factors of why people don't perform. So, let's take it from the top!

JOE

SCENRIO 1.

DOES THIS PERSON KNOW WHAT THEY'RE SUPPOSED TO BE DOING AND WHY YOU WANT THEM TO DO IT?

This is the easiest one of them all. If we explore Lean Manufacturing principles, this is what we call defining the **standard work** in our Business Operating System (BOS). In Prosci's ADKAR acronym, this is the **A** for raising **awareness** for what you want to do. In Six Sigma—this is **define** in the DMAIC acronym. Simply put, you can't expect people to do something when they don't know what it is you want them to do.

Our (unwritten) standard work says that employee time sheets are to be submitted by the end of the second-to-the-last day of the month, provided that it does not fall on a weekend. Joe has been repeatedly late.

In our performance-diagnostic approach, a very simple, performance-correcting conversation might go something like this:

YOU: "Joe—I've noticed that you haven't been getting your time sheets in on time for the last several months. It's messing with the end-of-month deadline that I'm supposed to meet. Just wanted to figure out what's up. Can we talk about it?"

JOE: "Oh! I thought they were due by the end of the day on the last day of the month. Isn't that when they're due?"

YOU: "Oh! Well, that explains it! Nope, they're due on the second to the last business day that's closest to the end of the month."

JOE: "Oh, no problem then. I thought they were due the last day of the month. I'll do them a day earlier. Sorry!"

IT STARTS WITH ONE.

Easy enough, right? You would be surprised how many times we, as leaders, perceive a performance deficiency when in fact, a person just doesn't have the correct understanding of what is expected.

Often work expectations are defined and well communicated at the time of implementation but then later communicated through word of mouth, ad-hoc informal training, and peer knowledge transfer. If your organization has even average turnover in particular jobs, it is quite possible that people could legitimately not know what a particular policy, procedure, or quality standard is.

Proactively stated: If you want people to perform, be sure your team knows what you want them to do, and to the standard you want them to do it.

JOE

SCENARIO 2.

DOES THE TECHNOLOGY AND/OR OTHER PROCESSES YOU'RE ASKING THIS PERSON TO USE ALIGN NICELY WITH THE NEW CHANGE?

This one is a little tougher and is sometimes a little tougher to correct because the corrective action might be on you as the leader, and it may involve others. It is a classic case that happens all the time.

Often, we define standard work that works nicely for one group but doesn't work so nicely for some of the contributors and doesn't take into consideration some nuances. Sometimes these changes build complexity into the technology solutions that we expect people to use, creating a barrier to adoption. Sometimes the process works fine for one scenario but not for another scenario.

Let's continue with Joe and his time sheet, but this time experience it from a slightly different perspective.

YOU: "Joe, I've noticed that you haven't been getting your time sheets in on time for the last several months. It's messing with the end-of-month deadline that I'm supposed to meet. Just wanted to figure out what's up. Can we talk about it?"

JOE: "Sure. What's up?"

YOU: "I've been getting your time sheets at the end of the day on the last day of the end of the month, but they're actually due the day before, so I can have time to roll them up. My reports are due by the end of day on the last day of the month, so I've been doing them in the evenings."

JOE: "Oh gosh! I'm sorry it's messing with your evenings, and I'm doing my best to get them in. I've been pulling together my time sheets a couple days earlier, actually, but one of the project managers I've been doing work for has been added as one of the approvers on my time sheet, and I don't think it actually submits to you until she's had an opportunity to approve my time. I think this has caused some delays for you. I've tried to follow up, but it hasn't been working very well. Any suggestions?"

YOU: "Oh, that makes sense. I didn't realize you had other approvers. Let me look into it and see what I can do. Thanks for trying to do it early, though!"

In this scenario, it was not Joe's performance deficiency, but another process and some technology had been put in place to ensure time approval for a single project that contributed to the perception of Joe's delay. Actually, the secondary approver was probably the root cause of the delay, but she might not have been aware of the downstream impact of approval timing.

This is a simplistic example, but organizations come up with great new changes to processes and expectations all the time without exploring how they align with other sub-processes or technology.

Proactively stated: If you want people to perform, ensure that the processes and technology are aligned so that people can efficiently and effectively achieve the objective.

JOE

SCENARIO 3.

DOES THIS PERSON KNOW HOW TO DO WHAT YOU'RE ASKING THEM TO DO?

If the answer to this question is no, then it is appropriate to arrange training, coaching, or some sort of skill reinforcement until this person does know how to complete the work. Of the seven factors that impact successful performance for the individual contributor, this is the only one where introducing training is appropriate.

In fact, in the instructional design world, we used to say, "If someone's life depended on performing the task to the desired standard, would they live?" If the answer is yes, then they *probably know* how to do what you're asking them to do. If the answer is no, then more training is appropriate. I tend to feel that this statement is a little harsh, and that there may be some gray area. For instance, maybe they know how to do it, but maybe not in the most efficient way, so performing the task is excruciatingly time-consuming. With a little reinforcement, though, you may be able to introduce some more efficient practices.

OK. Back to Joe, his time sheet, and a different variation.

You: "Joe—I've noticed that you haven't been getting your time sheets in on time for the last several months. It's messing with the end-of-month deadline that I'm supposed to meet. Just wanted to figure out what's up. Can we talk about it?"

JOE: "Sure. What's up?"

YOU: "I've been getting your time sheets at the end of the day on the last day of the end of the month, but they're actually due the day before, so I can have time to roll them up. My reports are due by the end of day on the last day of the month, so I've been doing them in the evenings."

JOE: "Oh gosh! Sorry about your evenings. Honestly, we started using this new timekeeping program a few months ago, and it feels so much more complex than simply doing it in a spreadsheet. I feel like I have to manually enter every task and project, and it is honestly taking forever to do. Is there a way to upload a spreadsheet or something? I feel like I'm starting early, but I feel like I must be missing something. Are other people having success with this program?"

YOU: "Ouch. Actually, I've heard good things about the new program, but mostly because people like the mobile time sheet entry mode and the template upload option. It sounds to me like you might be adding each activity as a separate time entry, and I imagine that is taking you forever. Have you tried either of those features? I think there was an e-learning module on it when we rolled it out."

JOE: "No! I haven't been using either of those things. And I confess that I didn't do the full e-learning. Sounds like I probably should have! I'll see if I can find the link."

YOU: "Oh, that explains a lot. I know e-learning can be rough, but this one was pretty good—I think it'll pay off for you, and I'm guessing you'll *really like* the upload feature. Let me know if you need me to send you the link again."

In this example, Joe knew what was expected of him, and he knew one way to do the work. He was able to complete the task, but was not able to do so efficiently, within a reasonable amount of time. In this case, Joe simply didn't know how to perform this task in the most efficient manner, so training, coaching, and/or reinforcement were appropriate.

I see this happen really often, especially across generations. Younger generations have been working with technology since they could interact with it. I watched my two-year-old grandniece figure out how to play Baby Shark on her mom's iPhone yesterday. When I was two, my parents were excited when I learned how to whack the side of the TV when the picture was fuzzy, so they didn't have to get up and walk across the room to go do it.

Wherever you fall on the generational spectrum, know that not everyone has the same relationship with learning. For some of you beloved Millennials, not everyone just figures it out as intuitively as you do…and that doesn't make us less intelligent or auditorily challenged. And to some of you, just as beloved Boomers and Gen Xers—not everyone needs to have the step-by-step spelled out in the same way that we do. This is a time of very targeted and individualized training. Just like our preferred pronouns, we all have our preferred learning styles.

IT STARTS WITH ONE.

Proactively stated: If you want people to perform, you need to ensure that they know how to do the task. They need to have the resources available to them, and some people might take a little more time and practice to become proficient in their skill.

JOE

SCENARIO 4.

DOES ANYONE KNOW IF THIS PERSON IS PERFORMING IN THE DESIRED WAY? DOES ANYONE CARE?

This factor is all about accountability and measurement. People sometimes choose not to do tasks if they think they're a waste of time, especially if nobody is paying attention to whether it gets done. It is important to note that not all desired changes require systems of accountability or metrics. But when you're experiencing sluggish adoption or you're seeing lackluster performance, perhaps it is because people perceive that the task isn't that important, or maybe it was important at one point, but is no longer.

Right now, we're focusing on promoting accountability for an individual performer. Later, we'll focus on how we can build systems of accountability that transparently communicate progress to ensure that everyone knows how they're contributing.

But we should finish our example. Back to Joe, his time sheet, and a different variation.

YOU: "Joe—I've noticed that you haven't been getting your time sheets in on time for the last several months. It's messing with the end-of-month deadline that I'm supposed to meet. I've been doing them in the evenings. Just wanted to figure out what's up. Can we talk about it?"

JOE: "Sure! Sorry! I didn't even think they were that important. I thought we were just doing time sheets for a few months so we could do that time study. I didn't realize you had an end-of-month deadline. So, are we doing them indefinitely now?"

IT STARTS WITH ONE.

YOU: "Yep. I know it takes a few more minutes for you guys, but the results of the time study were pretty eye opening in terms of where we have been spending our time and resources. We're going to keep doing it indefinitely."

JOE: "Sounds good. I'll keep doing it, then, and get them in a day earlier. Oh, and sorry for the evening work, I didn't realize I was impacting your day!"

Accountability goes hand in hand with making sure that people know what is expected. Sometimes people need a reminder. Issuing reminders or recognizing people for positive performance in a group or team meeting setting is often an easy way to reinforce an expectation, and this case probably would have sufficed for reminding Joe. Just bringing the situation up in conversation raises the awareness of the expectation and creates the accountability, thus addressing the performance deficiency here.

Proactively stated: If you want people to perform, you may need to reiterate the importance of what you're asking them to do, and in some cases, even transparently display related metrics or dashboards. This sort of reminder creates accountability.

Like defining the work or expectation, sometimes we're pretty good at discussing, creating accountability, and highlighting results when a new change is implemented, but when our focus falls off...sometimes so does the focus of individuals.

JOE

SCENARIO 5.

IS THIS PERSON BEING REWARDED FOR POOR PERFORMANCE OR PUNISHED FOR ADHERING TO THE PROCESS OR DESIRED BEHAVIOR?

Often organizational leaders have a great idea for implementing a new process, procedure, tool, or expectation, but we don't always do our due diligence at holding each team member accountable to the same standard or quality of work. Sometimes, those people who follow the standard work to the degree of quality that is expected are punished by having to embark on a laborious process that impacts the quality of their other work or their personal time. Alternatively, those who cut corners may actually be just checking the boxes, so they escape scrutiny, and they're actually rewarded by having the time back when they haven't performed the task to the expected level of quality or accuracy.

Sometimes our expectations are a much greater ask of some than of others, and we haven't fully evaluated the impact.

Let's play this out in Joe's time sheet example.

YOU: "Joe—I've noticed that you haven't been getting your time sheets in on time for the last several months. It's messing with the end-of-month deadline that I'm supposed to meet, and I've been doing it in the evenings in order to meet my deadline. Just wanted to figure out what's up. Can we talk about it?"

JOE: "Yep. I'm glad you brought this up, and I'm sorry if I've been messing with your evenings. I have to be honest; this whole process has been messing with my evenings, too. I know that this may not be particularly complex for most of the members of our team since they may have only one or two projects. But I split my

IT STARTS WITH ONE.

time between five different projects, and my time entry is really pretty complex. To top it off, the technology we're using doesn't have the right attributes to differentiate between my projects, and I have multiple approvers that I have to track down before I can submit to you.

What started out as a time study has really turned into a time sucker for me. Is all this information really necessary, and is there a way to simplify this for me?"

YOU: "Wow, I had no idea you were spending this much time. But now that I think about it, I can see how spreading your expertise across multiple projects could result in a particularly complex time sheet. Can we take a look at your time entries and see how we might be able to simplify? If I need to, I can discuss it with some of the other project managers to make sure the information we're asking for is truly beneficial, and not just an exercise in data entry for you."

JOE: "That would be great. I want to help you guys get what you want, but this has been a little over the top, and I'm not sure it is serving any great purpose."

YOU: "I bet. I'm glad we got a chance to talk about it, and I appreciate your putting forth the extra effort to be sure the time reporting is accurate."

In this case, Joe feels like he's being punished for performing this task to the degree of granularity that is expected. Because he's supporting multiple projects, it feels especially burdensome in relation to his team members. He has a point—and why would you want to create busywork for this guy? He's already supporting *multiple* projects.

You can also flip this concept to see how people are sometimes rewarded for non-performance. Let's say that instead of having a late, but complete time sheet, Joe submitted an on-time but quick, low-quality time sheet that allowed him to fly under the radar. He saved his own time by not providing the expected level of accuracy or granularity in the detail. In this case, he would be rewarded by having completed the desired task with minimal impact to his time. Something still gives, though, and instead of it being Joe's time, it is the accuracy of the time sheet. In the end, this still results in a performance deficiency, but it is due to the quality and accuracy of the time sheet instead of the timeliness of the submission.

Exploring the consequences is where you jump into your empathetic self and become *in service* to your team member. Would you be willing to happily do what you're asking Joe to do? Have you considered how this standard work might apply differently for some team members in comparison to others? In reality, you might not be able to help Joe out, and he might need to continue to provide his time sheet in exactly the same way. But having the discussion and making the authentic effort to understand his perspective will make doing it much more palatable for him.

Proactively stated: If you want people to perform, you may need to anticipate the complexity of the change and work to

IT STARTS WITH ONE.

understand the ask you're making of your team members. If you were in their shoes, how would you react to the request? Would you work around it? How might people be rewarded for not performing the task to your expectation, and how might people be punished for doing it well? Service-minded leaders work to understand, empathize, and remove barriers.

JOE

SCENARIO 6.

DOES THIS PERSON HAVE THE INHERENT SKILL SET NECESSARY TO PERFORM THE REQUIRED TASK?

As you can tell, most of the factors we've explored so far can be addressed with effective communication, realignment of priorities, fine-tuning of the process, or a little training or coaching. In this case, however, you have introduced an expectation that involves a new skill set.

We saw this a lot earlier in the millennium, when we had a large number of people who had absolutely no idea how to type or use even the most basic of computer skills. A spreadsheet? No way! During this time, I was working with quite a few sales organizations because gaining insight into your customers and salespeople in a way that aggregated the data real time was the goal of many visionary leaders. Many people in sales were nearing retirement age and had absolutely no intent or interest in learning how to do any of their work using a computer.

A software example is an easy-to-understand scenario that most of us can relate to but this factor also applies to transforming organizations when multiple roles are merged into one. I've seen product and service managers for customers merge into a single account manager role. This often elevated the role and required a level of business acumen or communication ability that some people simply hadn't developed to the level necessary for the job.

When faced with this sort of diagnosis, you typically have three options:

1. Help the person gain the skill.
2. Weigh the risk/benefit for this particular person actually having to perform the desired task and see if there's a creative way around it.
3. Help this person understand that their skill set may be

more suitable for a different role, either within or outside of the organization.

Let's play this out with Joe and the time sheet. For the purpose of this example, let's assume Joe sells high-end widgets and has been doing so for a great many years. He's terrific at his job, he inspires the new talent, he's funny, your customers love him, and he is truly a valuable asset to your team.

YOU: "Joe—I've noticed that you haven't been getting your time sheets in on time for the last several months. It's messing with the end-of-month deadline that I'm supposed to meet. Just wanted to figure out what's up. Can we talk about it?"

JOE: "Yep. I'm glad you brought this up. I am pretty terrible at using the computer, and my typing skills are *the worst*. I've been trying to do this time sheet thing, but it takes me forever when I'm typing with only two fingers. I look like a complete idiot in front of the rest of the team, and it is taking me hours to do this. I even try to do a little at the end of every day. I'm great at sales, but I honestly don't see myself picking up this technology thing. I'm sorry that it's messing with your deadline, though."

YOU: You have several ways you could respond....

    1. You could be patient and help him develop his skill: "Joe, I get it, this is a pretty tough change, and I've

seen you struggling a bit. You'll get the hang of it, though. What if I pair you with Lori? Maybe you can help her hone her negotiation and closing skills, and maybe she can help you become a little better at navigating the computer? Also, what do you think about taking some classes to help you gain some confidence with the basics? The team really looks up to you, and I'd like to do whatever it takes to help you figure this out."

2. You could come up with a creative solution: "Joe, I get it. This is a pretty tough change, and I know you've been struggling a bit. This time sheet change is the tip of the iceberg, though, because we are likely to adopt more and more technology solutions. That said, you've been our top salesperson for years, and the new people gain so much from your expertise. You've also mentioned that you're not too far from retirement. So how about this: if you write down your time for me, I'll see if I can get one of the people in finance to enter it for you. I think seeing your time up there on screen will help the rest of the team adopt the time tracker, too."

3. Or you could work with Joe to transition into a role that is a better fit: "Joe, I get it. This is a pretty tough change, and I have watched you really struggle. Maybe the job is evolving in such

a way that isn't going to be such a good fit for you going forward. I know that this time sheet change is only the tip of the iceberg, though, so do you think you're going to be able to pick this up? Or maybe it makes sense to start looking for roles/opportunities that might be better aligned with your skills. Shall I ask around on your behalf and see if any of the other departments have any opportunities?"

I won't go on with the rest of the dialogue, because depending on the approach, the conversation will unfold differently, but you get the idea. Authentically discussing your observations with your team members allows you to respectfully figure out the right solution together. Of course, sometimes there isn't a better-fit solution you can offer someone, and the transition to a different role means outside of the organization. But when you're having authentic conversations, team members typically figure that out for themselves, and it ends up being the best choice for all parties concerned, even when it is a difficult one.

I used a simple example to demonstrate a point, but this factor can get a little complex. I was once hired for a software implementation role. After being hired, it became apparent that my boss really needed software developer skills more than he needed a project and change manager. I absolutely did not have the developer skills he wanted. I also had not represented in any way that I had them, and, more importantly, I had no interest in gaining them. We had a very direct conversation about it, and I was clear that if he needed a different skill set, I would do my best to continue to support the projects while he found the person he was looking for, and while I looked for another opportunity. We discussed the problem and determined the next steps. In hindsight, for both of us—I didn't have a clear job description describing what he wanted me to do, and he hadn't taken the time to thoroughly review my qualifications.

Scenarios like this happen all the time in leadership, too. I can't tell you how many times I've heard sales leaders talk about how they had previously been great salespeople who were plugged into management without learning any leadership skills. They felt "thrown into the deep end" and expected to swim. Once again—common sense isn't common—it is learned over years of ongoing learning, improvement, and experience.

Proactively stated: If you want your team members to perform, you need to be sure they have the inherent skill sets necessary to be able to both learn and perform the job. If they don't have them, you should have a path in mind of how to help the person gain them. Or work together to determine the appropriate next role for that person's career path.

JOE

SCENARIO 7.

IS THIS PERSON MOTIVATED TO DO WHAT YOU'RE ASKING? IS THERE SOMETHING IN IT FOR THEM? DOES IT ALIGN WELL WITH THEIR CORE VALUES?

Ok, last one, Motivation. I love this factor because it is absolutely the *most important* one. When it comes down to it, does this person *want* to do what you're asking them to do? Why would they want to? What's in it for them? Would *you* want to? If someone really wants to do something because they absolutely see what's in it for them, they'll usually figure out how to do it.

This factor is even more important today than it was back when Pipe and Mager were doing their work because many of the skilled workers we want to have in our organizations today know they have a choice of where they want to work. They have an abundance of resources available to help them self-develop in their profession, and quite a few employers and recruiters looking for their skills. These people are in demand, so they can consider whether the change you're looking to incorporate is something they want to do and how what you're asking them to do plays out in their day, world, and value system. Today's workforce is also much more transient. People are not nearly as likely to work for thirty years at the same company. In fact, in many circles, it is better for your career to gain insight across multiple organizations.

In essence, if you want to attract the best and the brightest and want them to stay for a good long while, you'll need to be *in service* to your team members. Now more than ever, employers that want to keep their employees are very much in-tune with their experience as an employee.

Isn't that great? It's like a buyer's market for today's workforce. Even in a pandemic, while there are those who might take a job because they need a paycheck until the world settles down again, the skilled workers you want to hire and keep are still very much in demand.

IT STARTS WITH ONE.

There are two types of motivation, extrinsic and intrinsic. *Extrinsic* motivations are external factors such as being publicly recognized for being a top producer, getting promoted, (carrots), not having your boss breathe down your neck about something, avoiding being silently listed near the bottom of the production report, or avoiding being written up for non-performance (sticks). Rewards and consequences, whether they be intentional or natural, also fall into this category. These are not always contrived; some of them are just natural. Like—one of the benefits of doing your work well is that you get a paycheck or achieve what it takes to get a bonus...which for many is a really important motivator... and an absolutely an extrinsic carrot.

Today, though, many people are looking at doing work that is *intrinsically* motivating, such as the need to personally agree with it and understand how it adds value. People think, "How does this work align with my values, and how do I want to spend my days? Do I like what this company stands for? Is it an inclusive organization? Does it embrace diversity among gender, ethnicity, and religion? Am I aligned with the impact this organization is making in the world? Is the company I work for committed to sustainable work practices? How does this work fit in with the life I'm crafting? Does this organization support me?"

Many people don't live to work—they work to live! If you're asking them to do too much stuff that feels menial, unproductive, uninspiring, disjointed, undefined, in conflict with their values or simply doesn't make sense, these skilled professionals may start to look for something else. For example, someone who is passionate about cleaning up the world's oceans may not be ultra-excited about helping an organization known for polluting oceans to achieve their marketing goals.

In today's workforce (even the post-pandemic workforce) employees fire their employers more frequently than employers let employees go. Sometimes this is a win-win, such as in the case of a person who leaves the organization because they lack the skills to be successful in a role. But more often than not, when a skilled, qualified person walks away from your organization, they're firing *you*. That means your teams are going to have to endure the disruption and you're going to be on the hook for recruiting and on-boarding a new person. Doing so is both expensive and time-consuming, and these reasons provide a very good business case for caring about your team members' experience.

Every single individual is unique, and their circumstances are different. The way they react to change is different, and their motivations for adopting a change are different. Their feelings about employment are different, and they approach their job from their own unique world view. One of our jobs as leaders is to work to understand what is important to every member of our team so we can do our best to maximize satisfaction and ultimately achieve the best possible performance.

So when talking about why people sometimes don't do something that you've asked them to do, it might just be because they don't see the value in doing it, or doing what you ask them to do is somehow interfering with the kind of life they want to have or the values they hold.

IT STARTS WITH ONE.

OK. FOR THE LAST TIME, LET'S TAKE A LOOK AT OUR CONVERSATION WITH JOE:

YOU: "Joe—I've noticed that you haven't been getting your time sheets in on time for the last several months. It's messing with the end-of-month deadline that I'm supposed to meet, and I've been doing them in the evenings. Just wanted to figure out what's up. Can we talk about it?"

JOE: "Yep. Honestly, tracking this time has added a couple of hours to my work week when I average it out, especially since I often have to follow up on my approvers. Nothing else went away, so it has simply been an added, menial task. This was supposed to have started out as a time study.

I have no idea what you guys are getting out of it, but for me, it is the lowest priority in my day."

If it's a Thursday afternoon, and it is between me coaching my kid's Little League team and getting my time sheet done, my kid's Little League practice will win, hands down, every time. What are you guys getting out of this anyway? It sounds like it is cutting into your evenings, too!"

YOU: "Yeah, I've heard that from others too. The fact is, when we did the time study, we learned how our resources are being used, and on what projects. The data was eye opening and is giving us the ability to figure out what work is adding value and productivity, and what work is simply unproductive. I know to you it may seem like a lot of busywork, but to be honest, the data coming from these time sheets is helping me to advocate for you by either getting approval to hire more resources so we can spread the workload or getting rid of some of these seemingly pointless projects that are eating up your time.

I've been listening to you, you are so important to this team, and I know how important your time is with your kids. So, while it seems pointless and menial, it really is helping me get the resources we need to improve our team's balance. Will you keep doing it for now? I really do think it will pay off. I'll also show you guys the data in our next meeting and see if I can figure out how to simplify the entries. Maybe we can figure out how to make it easier."

This conversation could have gone a bunch of different ways, but it was apparent that Joe saw no value in doing the task, considered it the lowest of his priorities, didn't know how the data was being used, and didn't see anything that was in it for him. You simply clarified how it would benefit him—and maybe appealed just a little to his loyalty to you.

He actually wasn't all that concerned about your late evenings, because perhaps he believes you're an adult who is also able to set your own work-life boundaries.

Joe is often an employee who is influential, valuable, very productive, smart, and puts time with his family above pleasing his leadership team. He's a good boundary setter. To get his buy-in, he needs to be included in the why and maybe even have insight into the data. When you do get his buy-in, though, he'll serve as an influencer for the rest of the team because he's a well-respected producer. He is also the type of person you wish you could clone, so you want to do whatever you can.

Proactively stated: if you want people to perform, help them understand what's in it for the organization, for the team, and especially for them personally. You may need to share the data and the findings so they can see the value. Each person you're working with has a unique set of motivating factors, and you may be able to simply ask them their perspective.

WRAP-UP

Before we can move to helping groups of people, we need to be clear about why the individuals who make up that group adopt new changes or don't.

I hope that the multiple conversations helped to illustrate the many different perspectives a single individual could have when being asked to perform even one simple new task or behavior.

THE PERFORMANCE MANAGEMENT UMBRELLA— TACTICAL APPROACH FOR INDIVIDUAL CONTRIBUTORS

To summarize this section, I'm going to take all these non-performance factors and proactively state them so you know what you can do as an employer, for each and every person, to optimize an employment situation and performance for an individual contributor. When we take the time and personal attention to do this, we create positive intrinsic motivators that build loyalty, engagement, and passion among team members. Those factors bring a unity to our Symphony that we can't build into any kind of definition of standard work.

1. Prior to recruiting, take the time to develop a job description that describes in some detail what you want someone to do, and articulates the inherent skills and qualifications of someone who will be successful in this job. Use this to help you recruit the best candidate with the best chance of being successful in this role. Once you've found that person, offer them a compensation package that is competitive and makes them feel valued, and help them understand how the organization's capabilities and values are different from other organizations.
2. **Define the expectations** and measurable objectives that will help your employees know what is expected of them and how to do the work. You'll use these tools to communicate expectations, measure success, and build capability. People are more likely to achieve the desired outcomes and feel successful when they know what is expected of them and how they measure up.
3. **Provide training.** Offer a learning path for your employees. This could include a variety of different methods such as e-learning, self-study, books, sitting with subject matter experts, virtual training sessions, or even in-person classes.

People perform well when they feel their employers value them enough to support them and to invest in them.

4. **Provide informal feedback**. People feel valued when they are mentored and that someone is invested in their growth. Schedule regular one-on-one meetings where you can discuss new developments, develop a rapport and build a relationship. To avoid micromanagement, this shouldn't be too often (bi-weekly or even monthly is usually good), and I can't stress enough how much this needs to be a *dialogue* Coaching helps people build proficiency, autonomy, and mastery in their work so that they can operate confidently and independently. One-on-one meetings are also a great way to build a relationship, understand motivations, and create accountability. People who have regular (but not too regular) and effective one-on-one meetings that involve bi-directional conversation feel supported in their growth, valued professionally, and cared about personally.

5. **Provide formal feedback**: Most organizations have some sort of annual or semi-annual performance discussions to set goals and monitor progress against those goals Often, the achievement of those goals results in a salary increase or bonus. Goal setting is an excellent practice, and bi-annual, formal checkpoints help team members stay accountable for achieving those goals, while leaders stay accountable to provide the support necessary. When facilitated well, these can be an excellent practice.

Facilitated poorly, they can be seen as a transactional financial event, or even a de-motivating, punitive time each year where you learn about all of your opportunities to improve.

Formal feedback should be more of a summary of what you've been discussing during your one-on-ones. There should be no surprises, and for maximum benefit, should be a discussion around personalized macro goal setting related to ongoing professional growth and development.

6. **Build a career path together**. Sometimes there are obvious career paths, and some require a bit of creativity. Exploring career path desires and including team members in regular one-on-one and bi-annual discussions helps you to advocate for them, promotes growth, and builds loyalty toward you as a leader and to the organization you serve.

THE PERFORMANCE MANAGEMENT UMBRELLA— INTRINSIC OUTCOMES FOR INDIVIDUAL CONTRIBUTORS

To summarize these concepts, I use an umbrella. There are multiple factors that lend to positive employee experiences for your team members, and these factors create an umbrella. Not one of these factors can achieve your objective alone. It takes an approach that combines multiple factors to achieve this level of excellence. The tines of the open umbrella represent the tactical approaches we can take to create positive team member experiences, and, when approached as a collective, establish healthy performance management practices.

The intrinsic results of proactively addressing these tactics, and authentically caring about the team member's experience (often referred to as Employee Experience or 'EX' today), are reflected at the top of the umbrella.

People who are well suited for their jobs, are competitively compensated, are attracted to an organization's values, have well-defined work, have a good rapport with their leaders, are challenged to learn new skills, set goals, have accountability for achieving them, and have a defined path for their career growth tend to feel valued, interested, engaged, loyal, important, inspired and challenged. Those are very important intrinsic motivating factors.

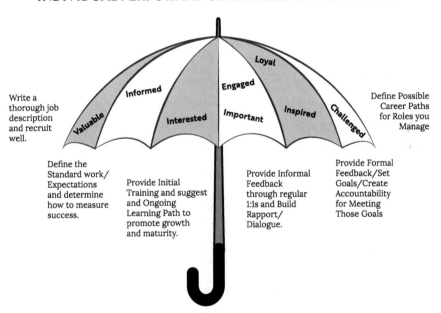

INDIVIDUAL PERFORMANCE MANAGEMENT UMBRELLA

TACTICAL APPROACH

We have now laid the foundation for our work. Do you see how you can prepare proactively and take a tactical approach to ensuring people are generally well positioned for good performance? Do you see how doing so leads to a more intrinsically motivated person? This is what I mean by being a leader who is in *service* to the people she or he leads. This is what I classify as good performance management for individual performers.

Imagine what it would it be like to be a part of an entire organization of people who feel valued, informed, interested, engaged, important, loyal, inspired, and challenged.

Let's see how we can take a similar tactical approach to managing the performance—or at least a change—for a whole bunch of individuals to achieve that symphony we've been talking about.

Chapter 3:

ONE TO MANY— PROACTIVELY PLANNING PERFORMANCE FOR THE ORGANIZATION

NOW THAT WE'VE TALKED ABOUT how we can effectively and proactively manage performance for a single individual—we're going to tweak it a little so that it applies to a group. The process doesn't change much whether the group is small or large. For larger groups, we scale our plans and remind ourselves that the stakes are a little higher and the effort may require some more involved planning to get it right the first time.

Whether the group is large or small, we need to ensure that all the individuals in the group:

- Know what we want them to do, and why we want them to do it.

- Have some sort of personal motivation for making the change.
- Have technology and processes that are well aligned with the desired behavior.
- Know *how* to do what we're asking them to do and have access to support or coaching to help them do it better.
- Understand what success looks like, and how it is going to be measured.
- Have an opportunity to discuss ideas and improvements to optimize efficiency and outcomes.

Piece of cake, right? But everyone is different! So how can we have a one-size-fits-all solution?

The answer is: We *can't* have a one-size-fits-all answer for each individual. But we can *anticipate* the most common answers to the group of diagnostic questions by talking to people. We can talk to other leaders, reach out to representatives of the various audiences, send out surveys, or even facilitate focus groups with small numbers of the people who will be impacted by the change. Using those most common themes, we can tailor our activities to proactively address these elements of change and guide our change communities successfully from the current state to desired state.

You may be thinking, "Yes, Tricia, that all sounds so great! And…we're a start-up, figuring it out as we go along. Seriously, how many organizations have you seen that do performance management well? I can't remember the last time I even had a performance review. Having written standard work or measurable expectations or formalized training is a future state vision for us."

Not to worry. The factors that influence why people perform are simply the building blocks of change. Your understanding of them helps you see why the elements of this model work together and how anticipating and addressing them has an impact on your results. There's no time like the present to get started! The next time you're looking to implement a change that is going to impact a group of people in your organization, you can set the stage for what "good" looks like, even if you haven't yet adopted any kind of formal performance management methodology.

Now that we have that foundation, the rest is doable...and is starting to become common sense.

To manage a group's, team's, or organization's performance, we'll use a slightly different umbrella. You will certainly see some similarities, but this time we examine the tactics to address the building blocks for multiple people instead of just one.

Similar to our individual performance management umbrella, we see how solidly addressing these group-focused tactics build a desirable culture that incorporates the intrinsic values that inspire people.

At an organizational performance management level, we:

- Define the vision and explain how it supports a strategy.
- Explore and address common motivating factors.
- Align process and technology to avoid barriers.
- Build capability through training, coaching, and reinforcement.
- Measure results, recognize success, and create accountability.
- Solicit feedback and ideas, iterate, and improve.

SYMPHONY

ORGANIZATIONAL CHANGE MANAGEMENT UMBRELLA
CULTURAL OUTCOMES

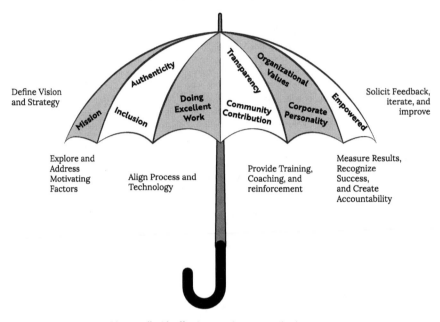

Manage all with effective, ongoing communication.
TACTICAL APPROACH

When organizations follow a proactive process for managing change, they tend to cultivate other feelings, motivators, and values that contribute to building a rock-solid culture that people want to be a part of.

Imagine a culture with a defined mission that values community contribution, that authentically values inclusion, that seeks and respects the points of view of others, that empowers teams to do excellent and innovative work, and that is transparent in goal setting and in sharing results. These organizations exist. Many of them have been intentional and worked hard at creating and evolving the cultures they have. I'm grateful to have had the opportunity to work in many such organizations with excellent cultures that absolutely experience the type of symphony this book promotes.

A STORY

When I was twenty years old, I worked for a company that did subscription fulfillment for magazine publishers. I can honestly say that I took that job because I was looking for a company that would give me health insurance for myself and my newborn son. This company was known for providing employment for unskilled people and teaching them the skills they needed to grow a career and provide for their families. They employed something like 6,000 people in our county of about 140,000 people. We did things like open mail, manage envelope inserting machines, process checks, print magazine labels, and answer customer service phone calls. And, of course, we punched timecards. I felt so lucky to have gotten a job at this company because I was a single mother with a premature son who was only a few months old. Because I could type *twenty-seven words per minute* and was able to clearly articulate a sentence, I scored a seat in the customer service call center for only $5.30 per hour. It was part time at first, but it quickly transitioned to a full-time position, and it gave me health insurance for myself and my son. How's that for motivation?

I can't even count how many other women and men just like me felt grateful to have a real job with benefits. Despite the low pay and the repetitive nature of our work, we loved that company. We were loyal and grateful, and it became a family. It had been an employer in our county for almost fifty years, and it took care of us. It invested in me. It provided training where I learned performance management, how to lead people, and instructional design. I worked there for eleven years, and it established the foundation for the career I have today.

Five or six years into my employment, the company was acquired by another venture capital (VC) firm that had every intention of fixing us up and selling us. After about a year of fixing us up, we had lost something. Some spark. That feeling of doing great work and supporting a community had been replaced with some defensiveness and feeling not-so-good about ourselves and the work we had done. The organizational depression was obvious, and one of our HR leaders decided to do something about it. He was going to change our culture, and he was going to take an inclusive approach to doing so. This was my first experience with proactive and effective change management. It started with the vision of an executive who cared deeply about the employee experience.

He communicated the vision that we were going to collectively define our values and build our culture. He wasn't going to prescribe it; we were all going to be a part of it in some way. He invited representatives of each of the departments and shifts to participate in facilitated focus groups at all levels of the organization. During the discussions, he asked us to arrive at what we believed should be the company's values and define what it looked like, behaviorally, when we were demonstrating those values.

He and the teams posted colorful, printed 'Living the Values' posters on the walls of our break rooms with behavioral statements like "Ask your colleague how you can help," supporting values like "Respect for the Individual" and "Effective Communication." He involved an army of leaders and representative workers to carry the messaging and spark the conversation. This campaign of living the values went on for more than a year—and it had a significant impact.

Our organizational culture started to pull out of its funk, and people were proud again to have accomplished something great with our collective group. A whole new energy and corporate personality emerged.

This talented leader had a vision, his team explored motivations, and we collectively built capability by providing examples and reminders of what living the values looked like behaviorally. He measured perceived success and employee survey results, he celebrated those results publicly, and he checked in during the course of the campaign to gain ideas and feedback so we could continually improve. He modeled inclusion, transparency, and authenticity.

The VC firm, aligned with our newly energized corporate culture, effectively improved our profit margin, and sold us to a reputable technology company. This opened up opportunities for many of us. Many years later, the business plan evolved due to changes in technology and media, and the company moved out of the county.

Today, though, it is almost twenty years later, and that alumni family still stays in touch. I would bet that every one of those people remembers the culture initiative.

Part II:

GETTING TACTICAL – LET'S DO THIS!

Chapter 4:

THE CHANGE MANAGEMENT WHEEL

NOW THAT WE'VE ESTABLISHED the foundation for managing change, let's get tactical. Let's do this!

For the purpose of this part of the book, we're going to transform our Organizational Performance Management Umbrella into a Change Management Wheel. Why? Because change management is often a cycle that fine-tunes and repeats until we've achieved the outcomes and engagement we desire.

I use a wheel because when we embark on a change, we rarely nail everything on the first try, and we shouldn't. It takes time and the ability to marinate in a new reality for a while before we can truly identify the best ideas for improvement. For example, let's say we're implementing a new time management process and some technology to support it.

EFFECTIVE COMMUNICATION

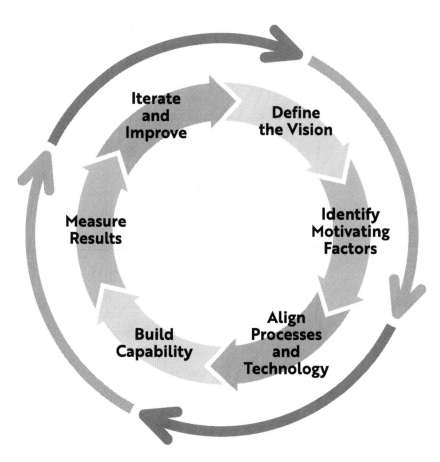

We define the vision, explore and address motivating factors, align the process and technology, and we build capability so that everyone is a trained user of the new solution. But it takes continued effort, reinforcement, and sometimes even coaching and collaboration to help everyone become proficient, mature users of the technology. So we measure results, address any hot spots, solicit feedback about ways we can improve, and arrive at the definition of our next vision or desired result. This is our next iteration—and we can keep chipping away with additional iterations or cycles until we've satisfactorily achieved our objectives.

Let me demonstrate this cyclical approach using another simple yet recently relevant example. Let's say that your organization has decided to implement a new virtual meeting/collaboration technology to enable your employees to work effectively at home during a global pandemic. This next scenario demonstrates why you might want to have a two-cycle implementation instead of just one. It also illustrates how change management cycles can be quick, if necessary, and can allow an organization to set iterative goals while delivering value early and promoting engagement and a positive culture.

In our scenario, the first cycle is to get the enabling technology out there and train people to be proficient so that the business doesn't completely come to a screeching halt. The second cycle will be to fine-tune, share best practices, improve proficiency, and build an engaging, collaborative network around the challenges and best practices of working virtually.

CYCLE 1

Let's start with the first cycle. The communication for the first wave might look something like this:

Vision: We're implementing a new virtual working solution that we think will cost effectively enable us all to work remotely during this challenging time. To get us all up to speed, we're going to implement rapidly. In two weeks, you'll all be proficient at meeting online, sharing screens, and going on camera so we can keep our business relationships alive while staying safe at home. Our goal is to be completely virtual in our interactions by the end of next week. To make this a reality, we're going to need everyone's help, commitment, and focus. We can do this! (**Vision**: by the end of next week, our entire organization is going to be collaborating virtually.)

Motivation

We know this time is going to be tough for every single one of us, but our ability to serve our customers and keep our business afloat depends heavily on our ability to continue to collaborate. We're going to keep our customers as our highest priority and do everything to keep our demand high. We're also going to do everything in our power to take care of our employees, and most importantly keep you at home, where you're safe. This technology will help us to do that. I know that some of you have to figure out a new normal with kids at home, and others may have less-than-ideal internet connectivity at home right now. These are things we will deal with one by one in the coming weeks.

These situations are challenging and are uncharted territory, so we will figure out how to navigate them together. (**Motivating factors**: Keep my job, stay loyal to my employer, serve my customers, keep myself and my family safe from exposure to a potentially deadly virus, be a team player, do my civic duty, etc. **Demotivating factors**: "Paint them red" and empathize—kids at home, shoddy internet connectivity.)

Align Process and Technology

We've already started testing this solution with some smaller groups so we can be sure that it meets our needs, is easy enough to use, and works well with our hard technology and security requirements. We've expedited our testing cycle for obvious reasons, and we'll be able to push out the new solution to you in controlled waves over the next week.

Build Capability

Our technology provider has provided us with a simple, self-paced learning solution that we'll ask each of you to complete in the coming days. We'll align the release of the learning module within a couple of days of your expected installation. Many of you are already familiar with this technology, others definitely are not. Please take the time to complete the learning and help each other out on your teams. We're identifying super users among all groups so we can have an army of people available to help you learn and practice.

Thanks for your patience and commitment during this trying time. Touch base with your individual managers to learn more about what timing and support you can expect for your team. If you're interested in volunteering, please let your manager know.

Measure Results and Compliance

(Fast forwarding a bit... let's assume it is now a week or two later.) Thank you for all of your timely attention to learning how to work virtually. Our organization has done an amazing job responding to this charge, and I'm pleased to report that in a seven-day period, more than 85% of our workforce has successfully logged in and participated in their first virtual session. Way to go! This is an amazing success, and we're learning more and more every day how effective this way of working can be. Still, a handful of you haven't yet reached that goal. If this is you, please expect a visit from your leader or assigned super user and let us know what we can do to help.

Solicit Feedback, Iterate and Improve

While 85% of you have participated and/or hosted your first virtual meeting, you may not be an expert just yet. We're all still learning, and practice and idea sharing will make us better. We're interested in learning more about your experience, though, and what you're figuring out about becoming a virtual worker. Do you have some tips, tricks, or ideas to share? We hope so! Please *click this (imaginary) link* to share your experience with us.

Cycle 1 completed!

Do you see, though, how it is going to be pretty important to have a Cycle 2 with a fine-tuned vision? This next cycle may even be communicated from a different leadership level, but we can't just stop at "Hey! Great Job! We're 85% of the way there! Yay!" If we do, we'll be leaving 15% of the people hanging, and we'll be missing out on an opportunity to build proficiency and drive engagement.

CYCLE 2

Here's what the communication for Cycle 2 might look like.

Vision

Last week we asked you to provide your ideas, feedback, challenges, and best practices for working virtually with our new technology and managing your home/work life. Wow! We were pleasantly surprised by both the number and the quality of ideas. Thank you. As a result, we're going to embark on the next phase of going virtual by rolling out some new, more advanced features like green screening (a professional background) and chat and polling techniques. During this phase, we will also cover some best practices for working virtually that we've heard from some of our previously remote workers, and from others who are just figuring it out. By the end of next week, you'll be a virtual working guru. You'll know how to display appropriate backgrounds, record your sessions, poll your customers and colleagues, establish work schedules with your family members to allow for consistent kid care, and adopt new meeting schedules that are more appropriate for these pandemic times. We're going to take our new virtual working reality to the next level. (**Vision**—We're going to grow in our proficiency, solve a few real problems by sharing ideas, and have some fun doing so through virtual collaboration.)

Motivation

Let's do our best to have some fun with this. After all, we don't have the commute. We're in this together, and we're probably going to be working this way for quite some time.

Do you have small children? Are you and your partner both working from home and fighting for internet connectivity? Are you working in the bedroom and feel like it's tacky to have your laundry on camera? Are you wondering how you can structure your virtual meetings to stay connected to your customer? We're going to spend the coming days sharing ideas for ways to help solve these problems. (**Motivation**: I'm stuck at home, my office is in my bedroom, my two-year-old is running naked down the hallway—this feels so unprofessional, and I'm losing my mind—I would love to share some ideas with others about how to make this work.)

Align Technology and Process

We're going to schedule some collaborative virtual sessions over the upcoming weeks to entertain some guest speakers, share some best practices, and keep our collaboration going. We tested having a one-hundred-person meeting this morning, and it worked pretty well! Watch for invitations to three meetings: one early morning, one late afternoon, and one in the evening. Of course, we'll record them in case it doesn't work well with your schedule. And if you have an idea that you haven't shared yet, it's not too late! Feel free to click the link to share an idea. (**Technology and Process**: Of course, you'll test, test, test to be sure that you're able to smoothly navigate the technology to share tips and tricks and review the idea submissions to be sure that they're appropriate to have on screen.)

Build Capability, Measure Results, and Continually Solicit Feedback

This organization might host scheduled web sessions, build capability, encourage interaction with super users, and continue to measure usage and solicit feedback. And, depending on the level of engagement and proficiency, it would determine the need to go forth with yet another cycle.

See how treating the elements of change management as a cycle gets to proficiency and engagement? Without a whole lot of extra effort, just a little of organization and focus—you'll be exceeding your goals for moving to a new style of working. You'll be taking the opportunity to incorporate supportive collaboration and build a level of proficiency and professionalism that will show in your interactions with customers *and* build culture along the way.

So from this point on, we'll approach change management as a cycle, and explore the elements of the change management wheel, one at a time.

A STORY

Sometimes, as a part of my discovery activity that helps form my change management approach, I'll ask, "Describe a recent technology implementation. What went well—what should we do again? What didn't go well—what should we do differently next time?" The number one thing I hear is that teams do a great job with communication leading up to the implementation, the training is good, and they get through the initial usage, but then everything just drops off. There's no one to call, ideas for new features or tweaks that seem to fall into a black hole, and leaders are on to the next big thing. I often hear, "It felt like we were drinking from a fire hose, and then the project resources all moved on." When the leadership focus goes away, especially at that time, so does the people focus. No wonder adoption drops off! What do we expect? We're hanging our people out to dry and asking them to figure it out for themselves.

If we plan and budget our change management (and solution development) activities through at least a couple of cycles, we're much more likely to exceed our expectations and gain really engaged people. The level of effort (and related budget) involved in the subsequent cycles is typically much lower than in the first cycles, but the impact on team member capability and engagement is significant.

Engaged people lead to faster achievement of desired outcomes and a positive culture where leaders and project resources gain trust, credibility, loyalty, and respect.

All of the elements of the cycle I just displayed become a part of a plan. Change management and communication plans include dates and milestones that are proactively established before a leader makes even the first, visionary statement. I've managed change management activities on a spreadsheet in a more "waterfall" way. I've managed change management activities using Agile user stories. Both work well. The most important part is that we proactively plan, allow for flexibility because plans are going to change, and that we establish accountability for executing the plan. I can't tell you how many organizations I've seen manage communication after the fact or overthink what they want to say so much that they never execute the messaging. In my opinion, the worst type of communication is that which never happens. Stay tuned for more on the communication plan and other tools after we explore each of the elements on our change management wheel.

THE CHANGE MANAGEMENT WHEEL

EFFECTIVE COMMUNICATION

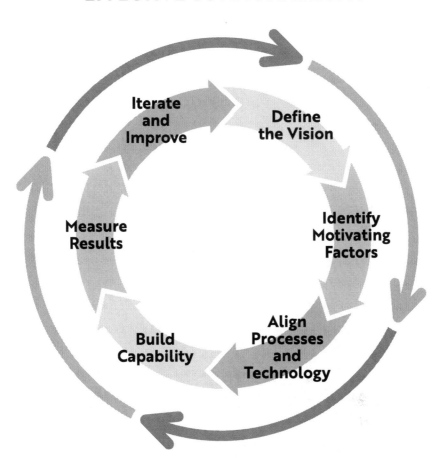

Chapter 5:

THE STARTING POINT— DEFINING THE VISION

SYMPHONY: OPENING NOTES

To set the stage for this chapter, I want you to imagine that you're a cellist sitting among a great many musicians, playing for your very first time in a metropolitan orchestra. You are sitting among the best of the best and feel really lucky to be working with this group of talented people. You are anxiously waiting for the orchestra's leader, the conductor—the maestro—to bestow inspiring words upon you and your colleagues. The words that come out of that person's mouth will make a big difference in setting the standards for how you perform this day, and perhaps on all future days of your career. It will be a day you will look back on in comparison. The words you're about to hear matter.

Next, switch gears, and imagine you're someone who has been playing in this orchestra for many years, this is, in fact, your eleventh year. Last season was pretty rough socially, and you've been wondering whether you should continue in the often-challenging life of a professional musician. You could never really articulate this, but you really want the person up there standing at the podium to move you somehow emotionally, relate to you, and remind you why you do this every season. You're looking for someone you can trust that will illustrate the standard by which you and the rest of the people surrounding you can become motivated in some way, to remind you why you love doing this. The words of this leader, if chosen well and delivered authentically, can put wind in your sails!

Now, you're the maestro. You're standing in front of this group of people. Everyone's heads are in different places. They have different world views, they've had different life experiences, they're experiencing at that moment a whole repertoire of feelings and emotions. The one thing they have in common though is that they're sitting there waiting for you to say something important to kick them off and point their energy in the right direction. You're their leader. In this moment, when you're addressing them this first time, you need to say something visionary and inspiring, something that these people can relate to and believe in, something that makes sense and is well planned and thought out. This is the first impression you will make on some, an opportunity to make a different impression for others, and an opportunity to expand trust for many more. As the leader, you know your words matter, so you take the time to plan them, rehearse them and do them well.

THE STARTING POINT—DEFINING THE VISION

If you can see it...you can achieve it!

I'll kick this chapter off with a little *Law of Attraction and Visualization*. If you are unfamiliar with the law of attraction, *please* Google it. Deepak Chopra in *The Seven Spiritual Laws of Success*, Tony Robbins in *Unleash the Power Within*, Jack Canfield in *Chicken Soup for the Soul*, and many others all have written about it and had some powerful experiences and outcomes that they attribute to visualization.

At the core of this law is that you can achieve what you can visualize. Because I have practiced visualization, have realized success in this area, and absolutely believe in this law at my core, I'm going to share it with you here.

As a leader, your words are powerful. To prepare your most powerful vision statement, you'll want to articulate it in the form of what you expect and *believe* you will see and *feel* in the coming months, quarters, or years. If you can have your organization, community, or team visualizing this outcome with you—think of the power the visualization of collective minds can have to drive the achievement of that vision.

That said, visualization is absolutely powerful, so you want to be sure you're planting the right seed. The *feeling* the visionary statement evokes is what really does the work. So you want to be sure that the message is authentic and inspirational for the vast majority of the people it reaches. If your message is meant to be manipulative or withholding some important truths or telling people what they want to hear, but you don't truly believe it in your core, people will see—and more importantly, *feel* right through that. Your words may provoke a feeling that is counter to your goal, credibility, and culture.

Some changes are more practical and may not require the same degree of inspirational leadership as others. Even something as seemingly unexciting as implementing time tracking, though, can benefit from some mindfulness about what you visualize. I could write another whole book on visualization, but I'll direct you to the books that have already been written by the masters mentioned above.

Let's take a look at some visionary statements that incorporate visualization. I'll shake it up a bit, though, and begin by embarking on an IT phishing example. Who *can't* relate to such a super exciting initiative?

As a team leader introducing a new IT phishing awareness solution, we might say something like:

"This week, we're introducing a new IT phishing awareness solution that will help us collectively become more vigilant at preventing attacks on our IT security. Did you know that 96% of phishing attacks are caused by someone opening an email unintentionally? These attacks put our brand, our customers, and our organization's data and infrastructure at risk. But we can prevent it from happening to us with a little heightened awareness and significantly limit our organization's risk. Last week, we did a test sample by sending a disguised phishing email, and 30% of us clicked on the link. So it's time for action, and it's my responsibility to help you to recognize these threats.

In the coming weeks, you're going to start seeing some email in your inbox that looks a whole lot like your other email, but it will contain some of the common themes of phishing email like misspellings, non-matching URLs, and requests for personal

THE STARTING POINT—DEFINING THE VISION

information that we would never ask you for. You're going to learn how to identify these potentially malicious messages, skip them entirely, and flag them as concerning. If you do click them, you'll get an immediate email pointing out your mistake. Think of it as a gamified way to raise awareness."

Six months from now, I'll review my end-of-month charts and graphs and will see a significant improvement in our malicious link click rate. My little bar graph is going to go from 30% to 5% in six months, and I'm going to sleep a whole lot better knowing that our technology is significantly more protected. We're going to be leading organizations in IT security instead of trailing behind, and it should be relatively painless for all of you."

As an inspirational leader embarking on a culture change, one might say something like:

"Three years from now our organization will be a model organization for inclusivity, diversity, and community contribution. The two- and three-star reviews we see on social media today will be replaced with four- and five-star reviews. We're going to read posts from our employees that discuss our programs, our organizational values, and the movement we're embarking on to transform our organization's culture. Our company will be highly attractive to customers, employees, members of our community, and our partners. I'm going to hear comments from you about how proud you are to be a part of this organization. This will be hard but important work and will take time to do it well. We stand for something other than just the manufacturing and deployment of great products or services, we care about the way we work, the way we treat each other, the experiences we have as team members, and the way we contribute to the communities we serve. I see goodness every single day, and I see so much opportunity as well. It is up to all of us to determine our organization's personality, which is why today, I'm announcing our culture initiative...." (You get the idea, right?)

As a sales leader embarking on a key sales enablement initiative, one might say something like:

"Today I'm excited to announce the most important change we've embarked on in sales in the last decade. This change promises to be a game changer for us. In six months, we're going to have real-time data that gives us important details about what we have in our sales pipeline, and information about our customer buying habits that will help us to target our efforts and work smarter. You, our sellers, will be working smarter, not harder. Within two years, we will have taken a significant bite out of our competitor's share of the market, and we'll be working differently. We have great products, we have the best salespeople, and we're going to continue to lead the market technologically, so we not only keep—but expand our competitive edge."

This first visionary statement for any change initiative is *extra* important because people have varying first reactions to the initiative. Clearly stating it will give them plenty of time to move through whatever emotions they might encounter.

Now that we've talked about incorporating authentic visualization into your initial statement, let's continue to add on and include a few other important elements.

THE STARTING POINT—DEFINING THE VISION

PREPARING THE INITIAL STATEMENT

Before we can fully execute and deliver our vision statement, we should have completed some initial discovery work and already explored the other elements of our change, at least at a high level. We should also have finalized the initial milestones of our communication plan along with any planned technical or process improvement initiatives that are aligned with the change. We'll want to communicate, at a very high level, some of the expectations of how the project will unfold during our initial visionary statement, so we'll need to have a general idea of milestones and target timing.

We don't need all the details, just the macro milestones, general timing, and some empathic idea of how the change we're working to make will impact the people who will be involved in making it happen. We'll talk about some best practices around discovery work and communication planning in a later chapter, too, but read on for some questions that will help you develop and organize your thoughts.

Content Ideas

Need some help formulating your vision statement? Try, at a high level, answering the following questions to use as an outline or worksheet. In the end, you may find that you have to choose the most important elements to include in your initial visionary statement to keep it pithy, but you'll incorporate the rest in some part of the communication plan eventually, so the work will be valuable.

- What are we going to do? (Define the work)
- What will we see, and how will we feel when we have successfully achieved our goal? (Visualization)

- Why are we going to do it? (Motivating factor)
- How does it align with our organization's values? (Motivating factor)
- What's in it for the individual contributor? (Motivating factor)
- What might be unpleasant about it? "If you can't hide it, paint it red!" (Motivating factor)
- When are we going to do it? (Technology/process/timeline expectation alignment)
- How are we going to do it? (Technology/process alignment, capability)
- Who's in charge of doing it? (Accountability/measurement)
- Who will be impacted by it and/or called upon to help make this vision a success? What demonstrable behavior might you envision these people doing differently? (Visualization)
- What are the expected outcomes, and how do they align with our organization's strategic goals? (Accountability/measurement)
- How will the recipients of your visionary message learn more? (Capability, set the stage for ongoing communication)

Organization of Content

Most senior leaders are either excellent writers themselves or have built a network around them that can help articulate the content in a way that is inspiring. If you're still developing your own style, or if you're a change manager wanting to support your senior stakeholder by providing a first draft, consider the following organization of thoughts.

THE STARTING POINT—DEFINING THE VISION

Keep it simple and definitely to less than one written page of text. Turn those same thoughts into bullet points with supporting images for any spoken presentation.

When I'm working with a new senior leader, I'll usually ask them how I can support them best. Some want me to draft the first version, some want me to provide simple bullet points that they can use as talking points, and some have ideas for other formats like pictures-only presentations aligned with speaking points. Executive leaders are generally very clear about their preferences. Some have me walk through and draft what I might say, and then they adapt that message to their own style.

Remember—this first visionary statement needs to clearly define what you're looking to do and articulate the vision for the outcome. It needs to address some of the most common benefits and concerns and a very broad timeline. It should introduce a person at the helm of the initiative who is accountable for the project's outcome, and it should paint a high-level picture of what the recipient of the message might be asked to do differently, without attempting to address all the details.

The key elements of a vision statement

- **Define the objective**, why it is important to you, and how it is aligned with your organization's or community's goals. Express it in the form of a future-state vision and how that vision will make you feel. Ensure that this statement answers the question, "What do you want me to do?" **(This part addresses the what and when.)**

- **Address benefits and acknowledge concerns** that are most commonly shared by the recipients of your message. Focus on what's in it for you personally, the organization as a whole, and for the recipient of the message (then triple check to be sure it is authentic). Encourage patience and understanding if appropriate, and express gratitude in advance. **(This part addresses the why.)**

- **Name the leader in charge** and express confidence in their abilities to carry out the initiative. Encourage the recipients of your message to watch for more communication from that person and encourage community members to reach out to that person with additional questions or concerns. **(This part addresses the who.)**

- **Close with a forward-looking statement** that includes reference to a requested behavior that people can imagine and relate to. Communicate with an appropriate degree of enthusiasm, encouragement, and appreciation. **(This part addresses the request and includes encouragement and appreciation.)**

Sender and Timing

The deliverer of the initial vision messaging is particularly important. In fact, it is probably more important than who delivers any subsequent messaging.

The vision message should come from the senior-most stakeholder who has had the most involvement in the initiative, can

THE STARTING POINT—DEFINING THE VISION

speak to it intelligently, and has some passion around achieving the outcome. Ideally, this is someone who has established trust as a leader and is someone people tend to follow.

As a change manager, you are very rarely the appropriate sender of such a message, but you are often the author of the first draft of suggested content that will later be fine-tuned by its deliverer. The vision statement should be delivered pithily, using language that is written at a ninth or tenth grade level (Flesch-Kincaid reading ease score). This is a time when I solicit the skills of one of my communications colleagues to edit my work since I'm usually too wordy. As a change manager, I typically draft messaging as a suggestion to the leader I'm asking to deliver the message. I ask that person to adapt and revise the content so that it flows naturally in their style of delivery.

Timing and communication methods for the visionary statement are of secondary importance to the content and deliverer but are still extremely important. The timing of the delivery should be as soon as possible after you've made the decision to move forward with a change, but not before doing some change management discovery, establishing an early draft of your change management plan, understanding the most common motivating factors, and defining high-level milestones and date ranges. Your executive-level vision statement shouldn't be overly detailed; you'll leave that to the leader of the project, but it does need to have some high-level time-boxing.

Let's say your organization is embarking on a new change that you expect to have completed by September, based on early milestone planning. Instead of naming the month in the early stages of the implementation, you might refer to the successful achievement of your goal in Q3/Q4. If it is an initiative that may take multiple years to complete, you might refer to a late 2022/early 2023 range. Build yourself some cushion with regard to dates because events happen that are out of your control, and you'd rather meet a time frame than change one. As your communication plan unfolds, your project leader can fill in the more granular details. The first executive message can refer to dates in quarters, halves, and in some cases, even full years.

In the end, pushing a date isn't the end of the world because people understand that it happens. Pushing dates too many times, however, tends to detract from the credibility of the team and the leaders. When you state a date and meet that date, it instills confidence and respect from the people you serve. Why not keep the date range a little broad when you kick off your initiative, and impose a checkpoint somewhere later in the plan when it becomes appropriate and practical to communicate more granular date ranges?

Delivery Method

So, you've established the initial vision, content, organization, sender, and timing of your vision statement. Now let's discuss *methods*. How should you communicate?

The answer: It depends on what works well in your organization and what kind of change you're embarking on.

Let's look at two examples to compare different approaches. If you're implementing a new process and aligning it with a **technology solution**, you might encourage your leader to announce it verbally in a regularly scheduled town hall style meeting, fireside chat, or all-hands web conference. This may be one of a few topics addressed in the meeting.

THE STARTING POINT—DEFINING THE VISION

In this case, I typically help develop some sort of visual in the form of slides and provide some bulleted speaking points. I also work with the leader to execute an email announcement as a follow-up to the verbal announcement made during the town hall meeting.

If you're implementing an **organizational change** that is going to influence people's jobs and bosses, you may want to handle this in a more targeted and sensitive matter that acknowledges the difficulty of the decisions and the importance of successfully navigating the road ahead. You will want to address this in an all-hands meeting, but you will want to be more sensitive to how the organizational transformation message might impact people by making sure it is the only topic on the agenda. You might also have follow-on messaging prepared for lower-tiered leaders to help them field questions in smaller group sessions immediately following the announcement. You will want to strategically time the personal communication of sensitive information so that it occurs before announcing it to the larger group.

In both cases, you may wish to record the sessions for playback by those who have missed the important message. I highly recommend working with the senior-most stakeholder to prepare a written executive announcement summarizing what was communicated in the virtual or in-person presentation and include a link to the recorded session.

When I embark on a change management initiative, the first thing I do is interview stakeholders and a representative sample of people in the community that will be impacted by the change. One of the questions I ask them is to recall a time or a project when they thought something was very well communicated, and what that looked like to them. I often get really creative answers.

This question has resulted in creating super short announcement videos, mass voicemails and/or text messages, branded email messages, links to videos, and presentations that included only pictures but no words. For the very first, senior-most leader vision statement, however, I recommend keeping the delivery consistent with the introduction of other initiatives of similar importance. This is the first of many messages that you'll include in your communication plan, so you'll have plenty of opportunities to experiment with other formats.

DEFINING THE WORK

Remember Joe? When we were analyzing the reasons he was or wasn't performing in Part I of this book? The very first example was simply reiterating for Joe what was expected of him. The vision statement is the first step into defining the work or telling people what we want them to do. We need to be sure that the vision provides enough detail to help the recipients of the message understand what is expected of them, at least at a high level.

Depending on your initiative, you'll answer this in different ways. But let's take a look at the visionary statements we started within this chapter and add on some text (bolded for you) that asks for a behavior change and is likely to evoke a feeling.

1. For implementing time tracking

"This week, I'm introducing a new time sheet solution that is going to help me analyze how our time is spent, prioritize future work, and level our collective workloads. Six months from now, we'll be viewing historical data in the form of detailed charts and graphs, and I believe we're going to have some eye-opening discoveries. This data will help me most effectively advocate for this team's tireless work, and more importantly, use it to align those efforts with the impressive contributions we're making to our organization's performance. Yes, this means that **I'm going to ask you to input your time into a system**. I get it that not many love to do that. I will commit to you, however, that we'll gain your input and make it as simple as possible to use while still getting the data necessary to help us achieve our goals."

2. As an inspirational leader embarking on a culture change

"Three years from now, our organization will be a model organization for inclusivity, diversity, and community contribution. We're going to be replacing the two- and three-star reviews I see on social media today with four- and five-star reviews. I'm going to read posts from our employees that discuss our programs, our organizational values, and the movement we're embarking on to transform our organization's culture. Our company will be highly attractive to customers, employees, members of our community, and our partners. I'm going to hear comments from you about how proud you are to be a part of this organization. We stand for something other than just the manufacturing and deployment of great products or services—we care about the way we work, the way we treat each other, and the way we contribute to the communities we serve. I see goodness every single day, but I see so much opportunity as well. **It is up to all of us to determine our organization's personality,** which is why today, I'm announcing our culture initiative. This is going to be difficult but important work, and I'm trusting Susan Schmoe as the leader of this initiative. I know she's been working tirelessly to plan surveys, focus groups, and meetings to jump-start our work, and **I hope each and every one of you will be willing to participate in these important meetings and activities** when Susan reaches out. You'll hear much more in the coming days, weeks, and months, so I'll turn it over to Susan to share our approach, our calendar of events, and how you can expect to participate."

3. As a sales leader embarking on a key sales enablement initiative

"Today I'm excited to announce the most important change we've embarked on in sales in the last decade. This change promises to be a game changer for us. In six months, we're going to **view real-time reporting and easy-to-interpret dashboards** that give us important insights into our selling performance, our customer buying habits, and most importantly, their experience as customers. This data will help us to target our efforts, work smarter, and serve our customers better. What does working smarter look like? As a member of our selling organization, you'll be **logging into a new system where we'll ask you to view, capture, and analyze data related to**:

- **Customer relationships**
- **Equipment installation**
- **Sales activity**
- **Sales priorities and progress**

I believe that within two years, this initiative will result in us taking a significant bite out of our competitor's share of the market and will **transform the way we do our work**. We have

THE STARTING POINT—DEFINING THE VISION

great products, we have the best salespeople, and we're going to continue to **lead the market technologically,** so we not only keep—but expand our competitive edge."

Of course, as we continue on through our communication plan, we'll become much more granular about what we want people to do. When we align technology and process and build capability, we'll be very specific about defining the work in much greater detail. So, we'll continue to address what we are asking people to do throughout the process. When we prepare to deliver our initial visionary statement, however, we want to at least include one ask so people can relate to an action, visualize themselves performing said action, and allow them to process the feeling that action evokes.

ENDING WITH A STORY

One of my favorite visionary statement experiences was with an executive of an insurance company who was embarking on a technology initiative for its many partner sales offices. He was going to be announcing the initiative at the annual agent conference, and he needed to differentiate this initiative from all others. He wanted to get away from the traditional "death by PowerPoint" approach that he had seen happen over and over again. He needed this to be different. We came up with an idea for him to refer to bullet points he held in his notes and make his points primarily by telling stories. On a floor-to-ceiling screen behind him on stage would be only a single, powerful image that would advance as his message unfolded. The pictures he chose were extremely powerful in communicating his vision and getting across the feeling he wanted to evoke. The recipients of the message appreciated this departure from the norm. He knocked it out of the park, received good feedback, and armed each one of the leaders on his team with bulleted speaking points that allowed them to carry the message forth in more personal conversations. It was like the best picture-is-worth-a-thousand-words moments you often see when watching a TED Talk. If you have an initiative that requires a new kind of creativity or impact statement, enlist your creative resources (try your marketing team), or consider hiring creative people online using services like upwork.com, fiverr.com or freelance.com to help you make it the most impactful.

SYMPHONY: FINALE

You're the cellist, again, sitting among a great many musicians. After hearing the remarks of your leader, you are reminded that you're sitting among the best of the best, and you are completely inspired. You are going to rise up to the standards of these high-performing colleagues, and you are reminded that your own gifts got you here. You have something to contribute, too, and you are going to work hard to be sure you measure up. From this point on, every season you start, you will listen for that inspiration. This maestro's words set the bar for what you're going to expect at the start of *every* future season. The bar was set high for you. Leadership matters...and you, like everyone that day, are sitting up a little straighter, intent on helping that conductor achieve the vision they painted.

Now you're that person who has been playing in this orchestra for ten seasons, and you are embarking on your eleventh. You've been struggling a bit with the life you chose as a professional musician, and the inspiring words of your leader just reminded

THE STARTING POINT—DEFINING THE VISION

you why you do this. You get to do what you love every single day. You get to work with people who share your passions and talents. These colleagues have, in many ways, become a family, and they challenge you to be better. Your work, and the work of your fellow musicians, not only entertains your patrons, but your music, for some, provides an important escape, a respite, a service. You decide that you're going to spend this year getting more involved with some of the other community music programs that are funded by your symphony's contributions. You have a renewed loyalty and feel grateful that the maestro's words delivered just the type of message you were hoping for.

Now, you're the orchestra's conductor. You were standing in front of this group of people knowing everyone's heads were in different places and were experiencing, in that moment, a whole repertoire of feelings and emotions. You were a little intimidated, just like you are at the beginning of every year. After all, you're just a human with a deep passion for bringing people together to play music for others. Who are you to bestow these inspiring words? You're not exactly JFK or Abraham Lincoln...

In the moment, though, you reminded yourself that you are honored to have the opportunity to lead, guide, and serve this group. You stepped up to the podium, channeled your inner Winston Churchill, and you took your role seriously. You planned, you wrote and tweaked your remarks, you rehearsed, polished your appearance a bit, and you authentically gave it your best. You prepared just like you hope your team will prepare for every rehearsal and performance. You created an excellent first impression, inspired some, expanded trust and rapport with others, and set an example for your expectations of preparedness. You held your head high, took a deep breath, and executed nicely. You won't know exactly how your words touched each of the members of your musical community, but you feel good about your delivery and the effort you put into it, and you gave your team the same kind of effort that you hope they'll give you.

Chapter 6:

ANTICIPATING MOTIVATING FACTORS

SYMPHONY: OPENING NOTES

We might *assume* that orchestra musicians have a deep, intrinsic desire to perform and to play inspiring music and that every day they get to work within their bliss. We might think they're lucky to have such a talent and even luckier to know what they were put on the planet to do. We might assume that they all feel incredibly challenged to take their 'A' game to every single performance because they're working with a similarly motivated group of high performers. In reality though, their motivations probably came, at least initially, from all sorts of places. Perhaps it was from a God-given talent or gift, perhaps it was a deep love for instrumental music, perhaps it was a gift and hard work that helped them to get out of a less-than-ideal socio-economic situation, perhaps it was from a desire to perform, perhaps they had a parent who hammered practice into them so they could follow in the family passion—probably it was a combination of many things. Over time, though, I'm sure there are plenty of difficulties that make the life of a musician challenging, and at times less than blissful, just like everyone else's. "Do I make enough money to have this be my single job? How does working almost every weekend impact my personal life? How can I fit in the practice necessary to keep my skills at their sharpest?"

I'm guessing rehearsals are probably not all rainbows and butterflies, and you have to be able to accept immediate, sometimes critical feedback. Your own internal feedback is likely often the toughest. Unless you're a soloist, you're always a part of, and dependent on a larger team. You probably play the same music over and over. I'm sure it can probably be a tough gig sometimes.

This chapter is all about taking the time to build trust, rapport, and to ask the right questions to get in touch with the motivating factors that are real for your change community.

A WORD ABOUT EMPATHY

Over the course of my career, I've observed that a key differentiator between those who are the most inspiring leaders, communicators, and change managers is the ability to anticipate and really relate to how people might feel about different situations. Managing change is very much about putting yourself in the shoes of others and working to identify with how they might *feel* about the change you're asking for. Working to understand these motivations helps us to build trust and rapport, to prepare authentic messaging, and communicate it in a way that acknowledges and honors those feelings.

ANTICIPATING MOTIVATING FACTORS

Think of the great orators, the people you follow, the people you're curious about. Almost all of them are able to humanize a concept and address it in a way you can identify with. You feel like they understand you. Their ability to empathize helps them to craft relatable messaging, and authentically carry those messages out to those who follow them.

Take Oprah Winfrey. She's a multi-billionaire, but one of the reasons people have followed her for the last many decades is because she's relatable. When you observe her interviewing someone, you can see her trying to get to a true, relatable place and validate what they're feeling. She's truly interested in knowing the back story each interviewee brings along with them. I recall when she interviewed the founder of Spanx (which I refer to as women's "suck-it-in" wear), she talked about the fact that she used to cut off her pantyhose, so she could take advantage of the control-top part without having to wear nylons. She may be a multi-billionaire, but just like me, she puts her Spanx on one leg at a time, so somehow I feel certain that we would be fast friends.

Barack Obama, in a recent address at a Salesforce Dreamforce conference, related to a crowd of 175,000 conference participants by talking about how different it is staying in the presidential suite, having to figure out how to turn off all of the lights with some swanky-but-complex centralized device, and confiding that he sometimes just wishes for the simplicity of a Hampton Inn and being able to just turn off the lamp. Being a relatively frequent business traveler, I can absolutely relate to having to call the front desk for some simple tasks like how to turn off a particular light, get the shower to turn warm, or figure out how to open the drain.

Warren Buffet also is incredibly interesting to me. I wouldn't call him the most awe-inspiring of orators, but he exudes trustworthiness. He's in the top-ten wealthiest people in the world, and still lives in the same nice-ish house in Omaha, Nebraska that he's lived in for the last forty years. He also goes through the McDonald's drive-through in the morning to get his coffee. And he does what he does because he likes the game of making money. If you learn about him, you read about his relatively hands off but visionary leadership style. His heart seems to be in a good place, and he wants others to come along with him and have success, too. Not only has empathy helped him to build an incredibly successful organization, but it also helps him anticipate how markets are going to behave because he understands people.

My new favorite Leadership icon happens to be a fictional character. Ted Lasso, played by Jason Sudeikis in a really amazing new show of the same name on Apple TV + represents the absolute epitome of a service-minded, empathetic leader. If you haven't already seen it, I highly recommend it! We could all benefit from channeling a little Ted Lasso.

All of these people attempt to connect with others by showing that they understand, share, care about–or at least want to understand others' personal experiences. This all starts with the ability and, most importantly, the *desire* to empathize.

The change you wish to see in your organization, team, or community may be smaller in scale in comparison to the changes these leaders address on a regular basis. But to manage the change most effectively, you'll need to be able to put yourself in the shoes of the people you're asking to change and consider how they might feel about what you're asking them to do. Your opportunity is to proactively identify the most frequently held feelings and

ANTICIPATING MOTIVATING FACTORS

acknowledge them.

Empathy is a Choice

Most of us have the ability to empathize, but we still have to choose to employ empathy as a tool. It may not be a natural part of our professional practice. For effective management of change, especially trying to understand motivating factors, we have to authentically try to not only understand, but really feel the various perspectives. If being empathetic is not a strong area for you, please make it a point to become more mindful and practice. There are more than a few learning options out there... just Google 'How to learn Empathy' and take it from there. It will definitely serve the people you lead better, and I'm guessing it will serve you, your friends, and your family members well, too.

The Dangers of Assumption

At the end of the day, we can be really good at empathizing, and we may think we're good at anticipating the common reactions of a team. Leaders sometimes want to bypass this important motivating factor discovery step in order to save time. Indeed, some people do know their team members very well, but it doesn't take very much time or effort to just ask. That way, you can confirm your assumptions, and you almost always gain an important perspective that has not yet occurred to you.

I cannot tell you how many times when I'm facilitating change management planning meetings and discussing motivating factors that a leader says something like, "I know how my team is going to feel, they're going to love it!" Or, "I already know how they're going to feel, so I don't want you to take time out of my team's day to get them to tell you what I already know." These statements represent huge red flags for me, especially if the stakes are high for ensuring a positive outcome.

I ask these hesitant leaders to humor me and allow me to, at the very least, organize one-hour focus groups with hand-picked groups of people in the various affected roles who will represent the positive and negative reactions constructively. I generally ask the more senior leaders not to attend so the group can have a safe place to speak freely. But I do have their anticipated answers noted so I can dangle them for validation if I need to jump-start conversation. I *always* learn some valuable nugget that helps us to craft a more impactful change management approach or at least prepare more relatable messaging. In some cases, this practice has resulted in eye-opening discoveries that significantly changed technology choices and/or change management approaches and thwarted potentially disastrous results.

A COUPLE OF STORIES

Several years ago, my team was responsible for leading the change management approach for a large organization that was about to implement a technology solution that would impact more than 8,000 people working at seventy-five different office locations across the United States. This was a sales organization that worked mostly out of their cars and served retail establishments. It was a huge undertaking for the organization, and the stakes were high not only because of the expense to implement a solution but because if the implementation didn't happen smoothly, it would cause significant disruption to the organization's operations and revenues. Because the stakes were so high, we were encouraged

ANTICIPATING MOTIVATING FACTORS

to make very detailed change management discoveries, which included doing ride-alongs with representative members of our user community. Ten of our team members split up and rode with ten different people for about four hours each. Overall, our team rode with and observed about one hundred users and questioned them as we drove. The experience was invaluable.

One of the things we observed was that these people were working locally on an offline spreadsheet-based application on laptop computers with limited access to the internet. Most had pretty good access to a cell phone signal, but the devices and connectivity situation they worked with represented a very real barrier, which was a significant de-motivator. In their current state, they had found somewhat acceptable workarounds using an offline solution. We knew that the implementation of new, cloud-based technology would need to significantly improve the situation to be accepted and achieve the desired results, not make it worse.

We noted as we tallied our findings that our project requirements had not included an offline version of the solution. Nor had we budgeted for any type of tablet that would enable both a simpler and more professional user experience, along with improved access to cell phone signals or internet connections. The team also had not figured in the expense of the wireless connectivity needs. We performed these ride-alongs at the very early planning stages of the project, so we were able to raise this risk to the cross-functional project team and respond to it far in advance of the build and implementation.

The result was the inclusion of an offline solution at the onset, and a next step cycle that would include the introduction of tablets and enhanced wireless access. This was a *huge* motivator for the user community and made the move to the entire solution much more palatable. Had we not taken the time to do the thorough discovery work, our high-stakes project may have resulted in an unthinkable thud of a reception by the people we hoped to serve.

Another time, our team was doing some change management planning work while we were exploring the budget and feasibility of a solution for a large infrastructure sales organization. Our initial plan had been to implement a pilot project for one 250-member region to evaluate feasibility. But as the planning unfolded, the scope expanded, and we were directed to skip the pilot and plan a full North American rollout that would impact thousands of team members. We had done a whole lot of work leading up to the change management session while working with only the single sales region. To do our due diligence, we decided to host some additional virtual focus groups to validate some of our assumptions.

The group we had targeted for our pilot fit the profile of super-smart, technically savvy engineers who could do pretty much anything but iron their clothes using a mobile device. One of the people I interviewed was twenty-nine—the oldest member of the selling team. When I asked this group about training and change management, they all said something like, "Not a problem. Our intern just implemented an open-source solution for us that we can use until the integrated solution is ready. We can use champions, do train-the-trainer, and rely on some self-paced training solutions. We're really good at figuring stuff out for ourselves...it will help us learn it even better anyway." The leadership all agreed that this team would require a minimal amount of change management and training effort. This was long overdue, and *everyone* was going to love it.

ANTICIPATING MOTIVATING FACTORS

But just because we have learned the hard way not to assume, we prudently expanded our change management interview efforts to include some other regions. Our work paid off, because we found out that in another region, not far from the pilot region, the youngest member of their selling team was in his late 40s. He described that while the people he worked with were brilliant engineers and could plan and scope significant infrastructure initiatives with the best of them, more than a few still typed with two fingers and were going to require a very different type of nurturing. So, once again, lessons learned!

Our learner profile was not to be assumed, and our training approach could certainly not be one size fits all. A figure-it-out-for-yourself, train-the-trainer system complemented by a self-paced e-learning module approach would have been a disastrous de-motivator for some other regions.

DISCOVERY WORK

Even though I list **Anticipate Motivating Factors** as the second stop on our change management cycle, we do this work first by anticipating and validating the most common motivating factors during the pre-planning and discovery work. Ideally some discovery work should begin before any project-initiating visionary words are spoken, so leaders don't miss opportunities to relate to their audiences. The themes identified during this early exploration and planning will give us the opportunity to advocate for our change communities by acknowledging and addressing motivators (or de-motivators) throughout the project and throughout the execution of the entire communication plan.

Discovery work can be done by hosting one-on-one meetings,

facilitated focus groups, and/or ride-along activities like the ones we discussed earlier. For representation, I recommend a 1:20 ratio of participants across audience profiles to get a good cross-representation of everyone's perspectives. When I'm doing enterprise or business work, I typically work to build teams that are inclusive and represent diverse regions, roles, genders, age groups, and racial or ethnic groups wherever possible. If you have a change that will impact 300 members of your organization or community, you'll want to gain insight from at least fifteen people. If you have a change that will impact 3,000 members, you'll want to gain insight from 150 people. Keep in mind that it may not be realistic to conduct ride-along type observations with hundreds of people, but you might be able to gain insights from a smaller number of ride-alongs and use focus groups to validate and improve your findings.

I like facilitating focus groups, sometimes in combination with other methods, because people draw on each other's comments, and you get a good idea of the group dynamic. They can also be done virtually, which allows you to include members of different geographic regions in the same effort. Facilitated virtual sessions should be kept to smaller groups (ideally under ten), so everyone has an opportunity to participate. If you're all concerned about the group staying positive, you may also want to set some ground rules to set a friendly and constructive tone.

Enlisting Your Influencers

One of the valuable concepts that I learned from *The Tipping Point* book is that every community has influential members that tend to naturally drive change, even if it isn't intentional. These people are often well connected personally to the teams they're a

ANTICIPATING MOTIVATING FACTORS

part of, and generally like to be involved. These people are doers and are often not the elected or appointed community leaders or managers of people in an organization. They are the natural leaders, though, that you know you can count on, who often wish to be involved and tend to motivate other members of the team or community. These influential people are great to have in your early planning focus groups because you can gain insight and stay in touch. They also often take positive messages back to the group and can be called on throughout the project.

These people are often excellent choices to take on a more active role as champions of the initiative during other parts of the cycle. If they are not a good fit or are already committed, they will certainly have suggestions about who might be good choices for those roles. So spend some time carefully selecting the participants of your discovery sessions. Having a diverse cross-section of influential and constructive participants will lay the foundation for a truly effective change management approach, and in many cases will be the gift that keeps on giving throughout the life of the project.

Painting it red: Let's face it. Some of you who just read this section are thinking, "If I were going to pull together a team that truly represents the diversity profile of the larger organization I work for, honestly, it will not be at all diverse." If this is you and your organization, then I challenge you to be the change you wish to see in the world. Inclusion is always better for the greater good, and I hope that you will pull together a team that truly represents the diversity profile you *wish* to see, even if you have to expand your numbers a bit to get the full picture.

Engaging Your Community Representatives

Regardless of the method you choose to gain input from your representative team or community members, you'll want to build rapport and ask some specific questions. This section includes a bank of questions I usually pull from, starting with the ten that seem most relevant for the effort. As the conversations unfold, other questions will naturally pop up, and I often find that I don't have to actually ask all of the questions to gain the insight I'm looking for. It's important to take copious notes or ask someone else to do so. It is also important to leave names out of the notes, as anonymous contribution tends to lead to more valuable input.

Some words of wisdom:

- **Do** pre-select 10 questions after having gained insight from project leaders or stakeholders and
- **Do** keep it positive and guide the conversation naturally.
- **Don't** feel like you have to ask all the questions, because you're looking to build an authentic rapport.
- **Don't** allow the conversation to spiral into prolonged bitching or gossip.

This work is constructive. While you want to understand concerns and acknowledge possible reactions, the interactions themselves need to remain as professional and positive as possible, especially in a group setting.

Before diving into your conversation, you'll want to set some expectations. You'll undoubtedly receive some requests or ideas throughout your discovery that you won't be in a position to

ANTICIPATING MOTIVATING FACTORS

guarantee will be acted upon. It's a good idea to acknowledge in advance that you'll certainly communicate suggestions and ideas, and while you'll have some degree of influence, you won't be the sole decision-maker with regard to approach or priority.

COMMON QUESTIONS

Here are some questions that I often use to guide discovery conversations. Some of these are more appropriate for technology initiatives, and less appropriate for community or cultural initiatives, but you get the idea. The intent is not to ask all of them, but to offer some suggestions that might spark some ideas for questions you might include for your own efforts.

- Tell me about you. Where geographically do you live/work? What do you do? How long have you been here?
- Tell me about the team you work with. How many people are on your team? What are the different roles? Describe the diversity landscape.
- I was telling you earlier about the initiative we're embarking on in the coming months. What questions can I answer about it?
- What do you think about it (the initiative) and the message I just shared?
- What do you think it will do for the organization (team or community)?
- What attracted you to the company, organization, or community? What keeps you here?
- What is the most meaningful part of the work you do? How do you think this initiative will contribute to that meaning?

- This effort is to really understand the possible truths of many, the good, the bad, and the ugly, so we can do our best to address concerns and improve the overall experience for people like you. That said, how did you react when you first heard about this initiative? Happy? Concerned? A little bit of both? Will you share?
- What do your peers, colleagues (or neighbors) know about this initiative? What have you heard from them, or what kinds of different reactions do they have? Why do you think they might have reacted this way?
- Think about another change initiative that you've been a part of here. What was good about it? What should we be thinking about so we can do better this time?
- Tell me a little about your day. How does it start? Where do you do your work? Are you at a desk in your office or driving around in your car or a bit of both? Do you work from home?
- What kind of technology do you use? What kind of programs? What purpose do those programs serve? (I also usually count this number because it is often eye opening.)
- How much time do you spend interacting with technology on a daily basis? How do you feel about that time? Do you feel like it makes you more productive?
- How will this change impact your day or productivity? In this context is there anything different that makes you either excited or concerned?
- Tell me about your manager or supervisor. How do you expect them to support this effort? Is there anything you think they could or should do that might contribute to its success?

ANTICIPATING MOTIVATING FACTORS

- Tell me about the last time you participated in a technology implementation. How did you learn how to use the new technology? What do you think we should do again or more of, and what do you think we should do differently?
- Think about the last time you participated in a technology implementation. After the initial rollout, how were you supported? Where did you go if you had a question or problem? Was there anything that you'd like to repeat or learn from?
- What are the best ways we can communicate with you? What are other methods you think we might use to communicate with others?
- Are there any other comments you'd like to share that you hope might influence our approach to this implementation or initiative?
- Are there other questions that you hoped I might have asked or think I should consider asking in the future?

Our work exploring motivation allows us to take a little of up-front discovery time so that we can truly relate to how our communities are likely to respond to a change. It helps us to be empathetic, relatable, and more authentic in the communication we craft. Caring about the experience and perspectives of the people we're leading is what builds the sense of achievement, makes people feel valued, and builds a lasting culture that people become loyal to.

Now, during these challenging and uncertain times, leaders have an amazing opportunity to acknowledge realities and help our teams to adapt both at work and in the communities we serve. Humans are resilient, and we're quite energetic when we're inspired. We can accomplish great things. We have an opportunity to truly change our trajectory as we come out of this pandemic into something that is even more focused and effective than ever before.

I want to close this section by reiterating the fact that exploring motivations is not about making everyone happy all of the time. It doesn't mean that, especially in a business setting, we're employing a completely democratic way of decision-making, and that requires that everyone is on board and in complete agreement. It is about understanding perspectives, authentically caring about them, and building rapport. If your objective and your vision make good business sense, it will probably make sense to your team members, too. Doing a small amount of due diligence through this sort of discovery activity will help you more effectively relate to your change community, help people work through any emotions ahead of time, potentially save you some unexpected agony or expense by not assuming, and help build a caring rapport and culture.

SYMPHONY: FINALE

Your symphony's players, like your organization's team members, have different challenges. They're talented, and they've opted into doing this work for a variety of reasons. They have a whole bunch of different perspectives that influence their abilities to perform optimally. As one of their leaders, you'll gain team excellence much more quickly by becoming in-tune to those perspectives and doing what you can reasonably do to respect, acknowledge and address them.

ANTICIPATING MOTIVATING FACTORS

If your symphony is in a community setting rather than a professional setting, your players are neighbors or constituents. Perhaps your symphony is being played by amateur community contributors instead of the professional, salaried kind. These neighbors and constituents have even more different perspectives about what they like and don't like, and may require even more flexibility and understanding from their conductor.

Taking the time to understand these different perspectives will help you to identify the true underlying personality of your community regardless of what you're trying to achieve. At the very least, it will help you to relate to people better, build trust and rapport, and help you and other influencers understand what it will take to guide the changes you're working toward.

Chapter 7:

ALIGNING PROCESS AND TECHNOLOGY

SYMPHONY: OPENING NOTES

Today, you're the conductor, and it is the first rehearsal for your new piece. You have quite a few musicians in attendance that will be playing it for the first time. The musicians are skilled, and all have been practicing their different parts, but this is the first time you're all coming together in the auditorium. You're excited about this because this piece is really important to you. You asked some of your team members to show up early to help arrange the chairs, stands, and any other necessary equipment. You talk with each of them about the people they're working with and learn a bit more about them. You even have some snacks and beverages—because who doesn't like snacks and beverages? You double-check the facilities to be sure everything is clean, tidy, and well equipped, and you even adjust the temperature and lighting in the auditorium. When people start to arrive, you or one of the others will offer a greeting or introduction. They feel welcome and important. Taking the time to set the stage for an excellent first impression is a way that you are demonstrating how important your musicians and their experiences are to you.

THE POWER OF A FIRST IMPRESSION

Moving on through our change management cycle, let's examine the importance of aligning process and technology.

This is about playing out your change to ensure that it works for the people you're hoping will employ it, and that they have the best possible first impression. Our job is to try it out with representatives of our change community to be sure that the new behavior or activity is in its simplest and most effective form. This practice minimizes barriers, anticipates misalignment of rewards and consequences, and also gives us an opportunity to gain important feedback about how we can improve on our approach and delivery.

When we're working with a process change that is supported by technology, we do two things to support the alignment of technology and process. The first is to work with our business stakeholders to define business scenarios and technology requirements. Later, we build test cases that support the business requirements so we can effectively ensure that the technology supports the intended process outcomes. The best testing is aligned with relevant business process scenarios and performed by representatives of our user communities that are going to give us rock-solid feedback. This may be the least intuitive of our change elements, but it is extremely important and requires the

ALIGNING PROCESS AND TECHNOLOGY

sometimes-difficult alignment of business stakeholders, change managers, and technology development teams.

Many organizations today have adopted the agile definition of a Minimum Viable Product (MVP) to define what is necessary for the first iteration solution. As a change manager, I must admit that this is not my favorite concept. Although I know that the intentions of agile project leaders are in the right place, the choice of words indicates that we are delivering the bare minimum. I challenge teams to adopt a complementary definition at the very least – how about the Optimal First Impression (OFI)?

There's a common image related to MVP, where the first frame starts with the skateboard, and then over time iterates to add on a pole with handlebars, and then adds an engine, and then doors and seats... I look at that image and say – why would we settle for delivering the skateboard? It might not have to be a Tesla, but shouldn't we at least consider something warm, safe and reliable like a Toyota Corolla? I do understand that iterative improvement is an incredibly important thing – but far too many change communities get stuck with the equivalent of the crappy skateboard with handlebars. So, give it a whirl! Next time you're defining MVP, shoot for the Optimal First Impression (OFI) standard you want to deliver to your change community when you unveil the first iteration solution during testing.

If your change is more about adopting a mindset or heightening awareness of certain behaviors or actions, you may not need to define or test technology, but you will want to return to some members of your champion group to pilot your approach. This practice allows you to try on your suggested activities or messaging with a smaller number of people so you can gain feedback about the desired experience before you fully roll out the approach to the larger group. This practice is thorough, and challenges you to get honest, authentic feedback so that the "what" you're implementing actually achieves the intended result to an acceptable standard and supports the vision.

To simplify our chapter, I'm going to break this into two parts: Technology Changes and Nontechnical Changes.

TECHNOLOGY CHANGES

To relate to this from an individual performance perspective, let's recall Joe, our time sheet guy. When we asked Joe why he wasn't submitting his time sheet, under this circumstance, he said he had been working on projects for five different business units, and for some, he had been playing a couple of different roles. He acknowledged that for some team members, the time sheet software was probably working just fine, but for him—because he was supporting so many projects—his time entry was a nightmare. This was a barrier to Joe's ability to efficiently perform the desired behavior, and it was definitely a disincentive/de-motivator. Joe was being "punished" for performance when he did the task because it was eating into his personal time. He still had the same amount of project work, though!

In our Joe example, he was on a small team, the stakes weren't overly high if the time didn't get entered, and maybe having a formal, proactive approach to managing change would have been overkill. But let's think about introducing a time tracking solution to a much larger group. What could we do to ensure we don't have a whole bunch of Joes who are being punished for performance or rewarded for non-performance?

ALIGNING PROCESS AND TECHNOLOGY

The answer: Include relevant business scenarios in our technology requirements definition, prepare test cases that use those same scenarios, and thoroughly test the technology with a representative group of user community members to be sure we're not introducing any unforeseen agony for people like Joe.

Before we roll out any new process or technology to a large group of people, we first define the technology requirement in the form of a business scenario. Then we test (pilot) the solution with a diverse group of users to ensure we are getting the results we're looking for without introducing unnecessary barriers. We solicit reactions from users about their experience, ask them to identify defects or features that aren't working as designed, and ask them about their feedback and ideas for how they might improve or streamline the flow of work. In IT projects, we call this testing activity User Acceptance Testing (UAT).

Remember those people we asked to participate in our discovery work? The ones who we thought might help us craft our messaging and change management approach, and whose help we wanted to enlist throughout the life of the project? Those would be *great* people to participate in our testing or piloting. These champions or super users are generally influential, good communicators, and constructive. They also represent a wide range of technical capabilities and have every reason to do a good job testing because of their reputations for being advocates of their team members. I also typically provide a definition of the work we're asking them to do before they opt in, so they know what they're signing up for.

If the change you're managing involves the implementation of new technology, I'll also encourage you as a leader to *advocate* for these champions. These people often do this work in addition to their day jobs. Their role is to test an *almost finished* technology product. Their job is *not* to do quality assurance (QA) for technology builders. To ensure this time is spent on validation, fine-tuning, and improvement, I encourage you to work with your technical project teams to ensure that thorough QA or technical testing is included as a part of the project plan to be completed *prior* to the user acceptance activities we're discussing here.

UAT is an overlapping part of a technology development build methodology and the change management methodology for the project. For change management, I cannot overemphasize the importance of this milestone. It not only represents our element of aligning process and technology, but it represents the first impression of the group who will be undergoing the change. It is an important transaction because it is when the most positive and influential people supporting your initiative get to take the new solution out for a test drive. When UAT goes well, and our champions have a great first impression, they take positive word-of-mouth back to their colleagues, and it builds *excitement*. When it doesn't go well, not only is the opposite true, but it disrespectfully wastes valuable champion time, it dings the credibility of the project team, and often adds costly delays. At the very least, it requires unnecessary rework on the part of the technology project team, and requires the testers to do rework, too.

We only get one shot at this first impression, so we must do everything we can to make it good. On our technology journey, we'd rather ride with the current than paddle against it, and ensuring the best possible experience will help us do just that.

ALIGNING PROCESS AND TECHNOLOGY

Performing each step of this journey well builds credibility and sets us up for success for the next step.

Truly effective testing, and therefore delivering truly effective first impressions, relies upon the ability to define, build, and quality check effective technology solutions. I want to acknowledge that the effective definition of business requirements in the form of relevant business scenarios that can be built into a test scenario requires a special kind of skill set and is not always easy to achieve. Too often, our project teams take the business product owners away from their day jobs to fulfill these roles, expecting them to write the requirements and/or step-by-step test scenarios. The result is often rushed or lacking in detail because it can be tedious work that requires an attention to detail that is not always possessed by product owners. Sometimes, we employ entry-level, less experienced technology associates to take on the tedium of writing down these requirements and building test cases that support them. The result can be somewhat generic scenarios due to a lack of business experience. Neither scenario results in the best first impressions and can cause technology change to fall short of achieving desired outcomes.

The good news is that I'm seeing more IT organizations employ dedicated product owners who are very familiar with the business but aren't pulled away by their day jobs. This allows them to be fully present to work with their technology colleagues, especially on more complex initiatives. Some organizations employ senior-level functional business analyst roles that have particular skill sets in aligning strategic business objectives with process and technology. These people are skilled in building relationships with business stakeholders, gathering input, writing thorough business requirements, and ensuring that they are aligned with detailed testing scenarios. They provide insight and promote growth in overall team business knowledge and improve the quality of both QA and UAT. These are exciting trends for the future of first impressions and the outcome of engaged and enthusiastic technology users.

A STORY

As a change manager, I was once part of a project team that had a change in mid-level leadership just after the project kicked off.

The visionary driver on the project left the organization with minimal notice, and a new program manager took on the role. This situation fell into the "stuff happens" category. There was not a lot we could do about it. The new program manager was eager to keep the project moving forward on time, within scope, and within budget, and he was very hesitant to communicate any significant risks, introduce delays, or depart from a very positive "green-light" project status. When we got to the UAT line item on the project plan, despite plenty of recommendations for delay from the rest of the team, he tasked a less experienced team member to provide some very rushed step-by-step test scripts so that the champion users could perform the testing.

During the first week of testing, the champions submitted almost one hundred defects on about as many test scripts. Many were duplicates, triplicates, or quadruplicates. We had not been able to achieve a successful demonstration the week before, but we asked these businesspeople to take time out of their day anyway, to take untested functionality out for a spin. To add insult to injury, we also asked them to use another complex technology process to report and capture screen images about defects that

ALIGNING PROCESS AND TECHNOLOGY

had also been identified by other testers. The whole thing was embarrassing. By week three, senior leaders from throughout the user communities were demanding appropriate delays and were forbidding the testers from wasting any more time until they had access to a system that was tested by the quality assurance team.

The good news was that we didn't roll out ineffective technology just to save our project stats. The bad news is that we disrespected so many people's time, and we generated so much bad press. The first impression was awful. By the time we actually finished the project, many months later, our stakeholders were less than impressed, champions were exhausted, and we had to provide training, re-training, and reinforcement many times over to achieve the level of proficiency we wanted. We were paddling upstream the entire project, which resulted in delays, scope creep to appease our frustrated business stakeholders, and a pretty significant budget overrun.

I will say, however, the team ultimately achieved and exceeded their goals. It was anything but a symphony in the beginning, though. We had a huge miss initially, and we ended up breaking our expected outcomes down into smaller chunks that were addressed through multiple cycles. It was so unnecessary, though, and so preventable. We could have reset expectations earlier in the process, re-tooled a bit, and reached that place of achievement much earlier. Had we just put a little more effort into pre-UAT testing and mildly adjusted our timelines to accommodate the departure of the leader, we could have set a much better first impression and ridden the current of engagement and excitement, rather than experiencing the exhaustion we got when paddling against it.

The moral of the story is that we need to define our requirements well and prepare relevant, detailed scenarios to help both our technology teams and user communities test them. We need to be mindful and respectful of people's time. As members of technology implementation teams, it is helpful to be reminded that our users, represented by our champions, are our customers. We *serve* them.

Why would we ever want to present our untested work to our customers to do our testing for us? That would be like going to an expensive restaurant for the first time, being really excited about it, and then being served undercooked food. Big disappointment!

Fellow technology professionals, we have an opportunity to provide excellent service to the communities we serve, and we need to be accountable for the first impressions for the technology solutions we deliver. The role of the user acceptance tester is to interact with already developed and tested features that are functioning at somewhere between 85% to 90% completion. The remaining 10% to 15% of work to be completed should be based on user feedback and usability enhancements suggested by our technology customers. Think of their feedback as adding the special sauce—or maybe the lovely wine pairing.

I'll hop off my soapbox now. And I do know that this is easier said than done...but when we're implementing technology, this testing step is a critically important milestone. This is our shot at a positive first impression and the difference between riding a current or swimming upstream.

ALIGNING PROCESS AND TECHNOLOGY

NONTECHNICAL CHANGE

Now let's use the example of some element of a culture change. Maybe we want to take on the challenge of implementing a specific change in our organization or community. Let's assume we want people to identify their own biases so we can better understand the role we collectively play in addressing problems with inclusivity and injustice in our workplaces or communities. This is big, important stuff!

To frame our work, let's use a fictional scenario that I made up as a mixture of a bunch of organizations.

I'll preface this scenario by stating that I am not an expert in implementing inclusivity/diversity programs, but this is a particularly important subject to me, so I hope to stimulate some discussion and some focused action with this example.

Our Scenario

We work in an organization that has been around for more than forty years. Our company employs almost 5,000 people and is the number-one employer in our small community. We require all of our employees to do self-paced e-learning modules through the Learning Management System (LMS) at the start of every fiscal year that bring the topics of equality, diversity, and sexual harassment top of mind. Each year, we also execute an annual employee survey.

This year we included a new question related to diversity and inclusion so we could gain some insight into our employees' perspectives. We included some definitions of the five key areas of diversity and asked a broad question: Given the definitions you just read, on a scale of one to five, with five being the best, how well do you think our organization does with diversity and inclusion? While the survey was anonymous, we did ask people to self-identify their gender, ethnicity, race, religion, sexual orientation, and gender identity if they were comfortable doing so, so we could gain insight into the data.

After tallying the survey results, we learned that the aggregated overall score was a non-surprising three out of five, but, when we further broke down the data, we found that people who identified as some of the specific self-identification groups scored us dismally low. The result was so disappointing and revealed a culture problem we didn't think we had.

Our CEO appointed a new Director of Workplace Inclusivity to dig into this problem, recommend action, and manage the change surrounding the implementation of these actions. This director pulled together a diverse but representative team of employees and leaders at all levels to do some research and come up with a list of objectives that would become part of an ongoing awareness initiative. The cross-functional team crafted a list of five objectives for our first-year change cycle. They are:

- Employ a self-assessment tool to help every employee identify their own biases related to diversity to inclusion.
- Provide an opportunity for every employee to participate in a team outside of their own work group to freely discuss their experience with the survey and inclusivity within the company.
- Provide a month-by-month focus on behaviors that represent a particular diversity topic and require managers to allocate 15 minutes of each regular team meeting to

ALIGNING PROCESS AND TECHNOLOGY

completing an authentic inclusivity discussion or exercise that is part of a "Let's Get Real" initiative.
- Implement a safe and anonymous reporting system to allow people to alert the diversity team of potential opportunities for focused attention.
- Offer professional inclusivity coaching sessions to leaders of people and/or projects at all levels of the organization.

OUR CHANGE MANAGEMENT CYCLE

Our change management work is progressing nicely. We've held our initial discovery sessions and our CEO transparently reported the dismal results. She introduced "Let's Get Real" as one of the top three corporate initiatives for the upcoming year.

She shared her disappointment in the results and in herself as a leader for having been so out of touch with what was apparently reality. She provided the vision that every single person in this company would be a part of this important work through a variety of different objectives, and with the appointment of our new Director of Inclusive Workplace, this would be an ongoing initiative so that we don't return to this level of what she perceived as complacency. She addressed the most common concern she heard from employees that the e-learning was a tool that allowed leaders to "check the box" each year and go on some sort of autopilot. She introduced the leader to whom she had entrusted this important initiative.

So we're advancing through our cycle, have conducted our discovery, and planned our milestones. We articulated the vision and have begun addressing the motivating factors during regular communication. Our communication plan is well underway, and we've made some significant progress on preparing our approach. It's time to align our technology and processes and "try it on" to be sure that we're not only achieving the best fit for our employees but remaining aligned with our vision.

Before we launch the assessment tool and manager-led sessions, we're going to talk through our implementation plan with our champion team to get their feedback. Then we might pilot the self-assessment tool with a different, less involved representative employee team to ensure that what we're doing is well received, well aligned with our vision, and doesn't present us with any unintended first impressions. We'll have an experienced facilitator host the debrief group to ensure it provides a meaningful experience. Then we will work with the leader(s) who are part of the pilot to ensure that they're well equipped to facilitate the fifteen minutes of "Let's Get Real" in their meetings with the pilot team. Next, we'll evaluate the timeliness of offering coaching or facilitation assistance from the core team if needed, and evaluate the effectiveness of the submission process (and related technology) for the new anonymous inclusivity inbox.

After completing our pilot group activity, in the spirit of authenticity, we'll debrief and ask for honest, transparent, authentic feedback. What felt good? What felt uncomfortable? How did it feel meaningful? What might make it more meaningful? Was the activity a good use of time? Do we think it will have the desired impact? What might make it more impactful? Is there anything you think we should beware of? What will you go back and tell your colleagues about the experience you've had here today? We'll incorporate the feedback that makes sense, and re-tool and re-test if appropriate. We'll move on from there, advance to our official launch and to building the capability of our larger community.

You see? This is important! The research we've done, the questions we include in our self-assessments, the facilitated debriefs, the leader's ability to facilitate regular sessions, the availability of coaching sessions for facilitators, and the agenda content are what make up the first impression of the team members. It gives our testers a full experience from which they can provide valuable feedback and further improve our rapport. This testing helps us to keep our fingers on the pulse of what is serving as motivation or de-motivation, and we have a chance to revise, if necessary, before rolling out our program to the masses.

If our champions and representatives have a good experience, or at the very least feel like they were a part of something that was well-thought-out and was authentically seeking their input, they'll spread positivity. We gain credibility for doing what we say we're going to do, and in the timing we say we're going to do it. If we skip this step, we have just significantly increased the probability that we'll be paddling upstream from this point on rather than riding the easier current of positive validation.

WRAP UP

We don't have to be perfect, but we do have to be as well prepared as we can be and do some due diligence to ensure that whatever change we're implementing has been thoroughly tried out to minimize the barriers to adoption. We want to simplify as much as possible, we want to minimize the possibility of punishing complexity, and we want to ensure that everything works well.

Maximizing the quality of the first impression is what we want.

Testing our process, our technology, and gaining feedback on our planned approach just makes sense and gives us a much better outcome. Trying things on and soliciting ideas and feedback from others *always* makes the end result better.

When I have coached facilitators before they're going to pilot a first event at a location they have never been to before, I always advise them to show up an hour early, deal with technology first (like internet access and projectors) because those take the longest to solve. Then, arrange your room and set your tables, strategically place any materials, arrange snacks and beverages whenever possible, and leave enough time so you can be completely present ten or fifteen minutes before your event starts. This allows you some time to meet, greet and build rapport with the people you're serving as they arrive. Pretend like you're hosting a dinner party. Be aware of the feeling your guests have when they enter your meeting room, just as you would if they were joining you at home. Make it inviting. Being prepared takes only a little more time on the part of the facilitator, and it demonstrates for the community you serve that you care about the experience they're having. If you put in that little bit of extra effort, so will the people you're working with.

These days, we have to figure out how to accomplish this same feeling and model of preparedness through virtual methods, but it can still be done. It just requires a little more creativity. You can still create ambiance at a virtual dinner party—and I'm sure there are some great ideas on Pinterest.

ALIGNING PROCESS AND TECHNOLOGY

SYMPHONY: FINALE

Of course, the first rehearsal of the symphony went as well as could be expected *and* was imperfect. There were some areas that will need focused attention, and you provided prompt and respectful feedback. You shared your vision for how certain sections can be played with more feeling and more energy. Members of each section offered suggestions, too. That's why you do rehearsals, right? Everyone was on the same page, though, and it felt like you were all moving in the right direction. You established your commitment to excellence, you demonstrated that you valued each of the contributors to the performance you're collectively preparing for, and you believe this group is going to deliver to a standard that even they'll be surprised by.

Chapter 8:

BUILDING CAPABILITY

SYMPHONY: OPENING NOTES

When I think of a symphony, I picture a stage full of talented people who have a God-given gift to play music. A whole lot of talented people who love music would be ecstatic to have the opportunity to play regularly in an orchestra, don't you think? To be able to do it as a full-time job and make a living at it, I'm sure, requires a whole different combination of dedication, talent, and commitment. While there are certainly a few child prodigy musicians who sat down at a piano or picked up a violin and just started playing beautifully...I'm guessing most musicians have logged hours and hours and hours of finger-bleeding work, gaining mastery over their musical talent. The players in our symphony learn and practice all the time. And then, once they learn a piece, they probably play it over and over again, leading to a new level of mastery. A musician in a symphony orchestra is absolutely a lifelong learner, constantly improving their capability by accepting new challenges and mastering their skill through repetition.

BUSY DAD

To get you in the mindset for this chapter, let's do a quick assessment to practice your approach and examine your own training preferences and maybe a few biases.

You're a busy dad who works incredibly efficiently between the hours of eight and four, so you can get your work done and pick up your kids at daycare before five. You and your partner both value your careers and do a good job divvying up your family responsibilities. Sometimes you need to work a little extra, but your family has a strict rule that extra work can take place only after 8:30 p.m. or before 6:30 a.m. You consider yourself a master at learning new technology and just learned that you'll be expected to attend training in the next couple of weeks. Do you prefer:

- The self-paced e-learning approach so you can prioritize it along with your many other tasks?
- Attending an instructor-led virtual class that will include two 1.5-hour sessions with a break in-between but will be hands on and offer the opportunity to ask questions?
- A combined approach, starting with the self-paced training, but with the option of attending an abbreviated instructor-led virtual class?
- The in-person, hands-on offering to be held at the office with the more social, idea-sharing experiences often involved with in-person training?

BUILDING CAPABILITY

YOUNG GRANDMA

You're a grandmother who works four, ten-hour days so you can care for your grandkids on Fridays. You just learned that you need to learn a new technology solution at work that is going to help you more effectively capture information related to your customer relationships and their buying patterns. Friday is your much-anticipated day with the grandbabies, but it is also the day that the training is offered. Do you opt for:

- The self-paced e-learning approach so you can do it on Friday while your grandkids are napping?
- Attending an instructor-led virtual class that will include two 1.5-hour sessions with a break in-between on Tuesday morning. It will be hands on and offer the opportunity to ask questions?
- A combined approach, starting with the self-paced training, but with the option of attending an abbreviated instructor-led virtual class the following week?
- An in-person hands-on offering to be held at the office next week?

LOYAL AND INVOLVED MEMBER OF YOUR COMMUNITY

You've been living in your small community for the last thirty years and have always felt like it has been a respectful and reasonably diverse place to live. You're active in regular town hall meetings, and you've been asked to participate in a pilot program for examining personal bias that may be leading to recently reported problems with racism and a lack of inclusivity in your town. You've been watching the news regularly lately and have been wondering about what you can do to take action, so you're opting in. Do you prefer:

- Doing an online tutorial offered through your city's new inclusivity website?
- Reading through a PDF with some examples, and a self-examination that you got from your city through email?
- Attending a town-hall-style virtual session with some of your other community members?
- Attending a town-hall-style small group discussion at a central park where you'll have small group discussions in a safe and socially distanced way?
- Doing the online work followed by a town-hall virtual discussion?
- Reading a colorful mailer sent through the mail from our city's Inclusivity Director?

How did you answer? I'm hoping you answered in the way that provided your own personal preference since *you* were the person in the scenario.

For most changes, technical or otherwise, building capability is about training. Learning how to do something you don't know how to do, learning a different way to do a task, or identifying your own tendencies which can lead to an expanded perspective or mindset, is all training. The variety of different ways to build capability all depend on the audience, the level of proficiency to which you wish your team members to perform, the amount of time you have to build that proficiency, the preferences of the learners, the inherent capability or experiences of the learners, and the complexity of the task at hand.

I started the chapter this way to give you a little practice anticipating the different perspectives your learners might have, but also examining your own biases and assumptions related to learning. Just like motivating factors, each one of us has a different perspective, a different capability, and a different preference. We might *think* we know best, but the best way for us to know the right answer is to *ask* so we understand common preferences and offer training options that serve the preferences of most. As with motivation, there is no one-size-fits-all answer when it comes to training, and we often project our own preferences as assumptions of what is best for most. Whenever possible, our best bet is to do a small amount of homework ahead of time so we can meet the needs and desires of the majority of our learners.

One might think that the technically savvy, very busy dad who is short on time is going to opt for the self-paced e-learning that he can do after 8:30 p.m. Yesterday, my son (who happens to be a busy dad with that rule) told me that he would much rather take an in-person or even a virtual course to get through the necessary learning all at once. He said that he feels like the computer-based training at his organization is worthless, and he always gets kicked out and has to start over, which is a huge waste of time.

I am the young grandma who participates in my grandchildren's care. I would probably start with the e-learning, mostly because I'm a connoisseur of such things and find them to be efficient. But I would follow up by attending a virtual web session if I felt like I needed more support.

Learning preferences are so individualized, and we have so much opportunity to serve our learners so they can build their own capability in a convenient and effective way. Technology has significantly expanded possibilities for learning, and in many cases, has shaved off much of the time it takes to develop engaging learning solutions, which allows us to provide more options to our learners. Some generations of learners may have grown up learning differently due to the availability of technology, but we shouldn't assume that more seasoned learners haven't adapted very well to newer on-demand options.

We can deliver training through a variety of methods, and we can build systems of accountability so that the learner is responsible for gaining the knowledge. When I started my career, we didn't have e-learning, YouTube, laptop computers, smartphones, learning management systems, or even PowerPoint and LED projectors. There were just a few ways to approach training and none of them, except for pre-reading, were self-paced. As instructional developers, we worked to develop a single curriculum to teach to the middle of the bell curve of a defined audience. We didn't have a lot of options. Now we have so much more capability to serve our learners in more interesting, efficient, convenient, and engaging ways.

INSTRUCTIONAL DESIGN, DEVELOPMENT, AND DELIVERY

I started my career in Instructional Systems Design (ISD), which was a tried-and-true approach to building effective performance-based training. I became interested in performance management because we were often asked to do more training to solve a performance deficiency, and often found out that lack of capability wasn't the issue at all! Mager, in his book *What Every Manager Should Know About Training*, prefaced all that he taught about developing training by first challenging us as leaders and training professionals to diagnose any performance deficiencies appropriately so we could be sure we were treating any problems with the most effective intervention. That work is what inspired my passion for service-centric leadership and managing change. Offering effective training *is* the most appropriate activity for the building capability part of our cycle, so let's dig in!

If you work with someone who is well versed in developing training, they'll probably be able to tell you about the most widely used process for designing instructional programs in the United States that uses the acronym ADDIE. The ADDIE stands for:

- Analyze
- Design
- Develop
- Implement
- Evaluate

In order to successfully launch whatever change initiative we embark on, we need to be sure our learners know how to perform their new behavior(s) to a specified level of proficiency. To do this, we're going to follow ADDIE as a sub-process to our change management cycle. Even if we're adapting an already existing curriculum or directing learners to something self-paced that already exists, we should follow this process, at least an abbreviated version, to be sure we've dotted our i's and crossed our t's. Let's take a look:

ANALYSIS

Analysis is all about gathering the information we need to drive our training design.

The good news is that we can do much of this analysis early in the change and project management planning process by including a few well-placed training questions in upfront surveys or discovery sessions with our champions or stakeholders. We can also explore any pre-built training options early on during our project planning sessions to align our efforts with those responsible for managing projects, managing change, building technology, or developing program communication or content. This way, we can arrive at a cross-functional timeline for training and launch. Again, just as in the discovery work that helped us understand motivations and reactions to the change, we won't actually *ask* every question, but we will ask a well-chosen few and gain the answers through conversation. Here are some questions commonly explored during the early days and weeks of a new change project that help us to determine our approach for building capability:

- What is the size of the group? How many people will need to attend training?
- What are the different roles we'll need to serve with varying curriculum? (For example, customer service representative, escalation queue representative, supervisor.)
- How different will the curriculum/training need to be in order to serve the various roles? Can we gain efficiencies by building modular content?
- What are our learning objectives, and how might we fine-tune them to ensure they align nicely with the business

objectives and technology test cases (if appropriate)?
- Have we talked with a wide group of representative learners and gained an understanding of learning preferences? (For example, self-paced e-learning, instructor-led virtual, in-person hands-on, a combination of options to serve multiple preferences.)
- Do we have any history with the various methods of learning and the effectiveness of the various approaches? (For example, if your learner prefers self-paced e-learning, do we have evidence that the method has prepared them well in the past?)
- Who will be delivering the training, or, in the case of self-paced learning, how will it be made available? How might we enlist a system of accountability for completion?
- What are the other key project milestones related to completing discovery, executing key messaging, conducting UAT, piloting training, and expected launch dates? How do those align with our instructional development effort?
- What risks do you see that may impact your ability to prepare and deliver training in time for launch? What mitigation strategies do you have in mind for those risks?
- What pre-developed curriculum do you think you might be able to take advantage of, and how might you tailor or customize the training to ensure relevance?
- How can you measure the learner's ability to demonstrate their proficiency once they've completed training?
- What kind of budget will be necessary to execute the desired approach? Which of the choices are nice-to-have rather that need-to-have options?

- If you were to plot training preferences on a bell curve, which would serve the preferences of the majority of the group?

In addition to asking the training discovery questions listed before, you also might take this opportunity to diagram the current state and what you know about future state processes, look through current-state training materials, walk through systems that are in use, and identify use cases or business scenarios that are relevant for your initiative and can be built into training examples.

If you are undergoing a complex change initiative, or one with high stakes, you may wish to hire experienced professionals, perhaps with subject matter expertise, to help with this instructional development process. You'll likely find that doing so will ensure a thorough analysis, definition of aligned training objectives, and development of a relevant, effective, and perhaps as important, reusable training program. Well-developed training programs provide a positive first impression for the larger group of learners, will serve as excellent reinforcement solutions, and can support future onboarding efforts, too.

DESIGN

After completing the initial analysis, you (or your instructional resources) will pull together all that you've learned to add another level of detail to the training approach for the design phase. A fantastic tool that can be used to detail the design of the training is a curriculum map. For the purposes of this chapter, envision a simple, colorful spreadsheet that details what we're going to teach our learners or the members of our change community how to do.

- A good curriculum map has at least five columns detailing:
- High-level modular objectives
- Detailed lesson objectives
- Supporting activities
- Suggested delivery methods
- Appropriate comments

If you're working with multiple designers, you may also wish to include resource and status columns so you can evaluate progress. Envision having multiple tabs on your spreadsheet using the same format to represent how the curriculum may change to serve different learning audiences. Consider your curriculum map to be the outline from which training will be developed. Ideally, this outline should tie back nicely to any business objectives and/or technology test cases we might have defined for the technology and process alignment part of the change cycle. As your instructional team begins to develop the training material, they can include even more granular details on your curriculum map and use it as a working document as the work evolves. Are you wondering if there's an example coming for you to look at? Indeed there is! Looking for more information on curriculum maps? Find a discussion of the various tools in Chapter 12, or on the Symphony Method website (thesymphonymethod.com).

DEVELOP

Once you've completed and summarized your analysis and detailed your design to ensure that it is well aligned with desired outcomes—you're ready to develop your training (or enlist the support of your instructional design colleagues to do so).

I recommend using blended learning that utilizes multiple delivery methods. Using blended learning is often the most effective when attending to very large groups of people because it offers options and addresses the preferences of the majority of users.

The most effective training follows a tell-show-do approach that appeals to three different learning styles. Each of us has a dominant or preferred learning style, though we can each learn at least a little bit using each of the others. Most people identify with being kinesthetic or hands-on learners. The second most common is the visual learning group, and the smallest number of people identify with being primarily auditory learners. The most effective delivery methods incorporate all three learning styles and repeat the hands-on experience multiple (I like three) times to provide some practice and build proficiency. The tell-show-do approach means:

- Telling the learner what you're going to show them (appeals to the auditory learner)
- Showing them how to do it using a demonstration (appeals to the visual learner)
- Allowing them to do it by providing a hands-on exercise (appeals to the kinesthetic learner)
- Debriefing by reinforcing what they can now do (provides repetition and builds confidence)

The reason hands-on, face-to-face, instructor-led training is so effective is that it incorporates all three approaches and allows the instructor to easily walk around the room to observe and provide real-time feedback. When facilitated well, in-person training can also be engaging and personal, which allows the learner to more actively participate in their learning.

Virtual instructor-led training is a close second, especially if it engages learners by directing them to participate in relevant hands-on activities. It is more difficult for instructors to observe the work of all participants using a virtual method, though there are some technologies that offer the opportunity for instructors to pop in and view screens. Virtual learning, when well developed, does allow an instructor to appeal to all learning styles using the tell-show-do approach.

Interactive e-learning is third because you can simulate the tell-show-do approach and can provide immediate feedback in the form of error messages. This is a little less personal and takes more time and resources to develop. But done well, it can be ideal for introducing simple concepts to large groups where you can gain some economies of scale.

Certainly, our nation and those across the globe had a crash course in distance (virtual) learning during the COVID-19 pandemic. Regardless of your personal learning preferences and styles, the pandemic has shown us that if we really want to learn something, we can figure it out. It will be interesting to see how learning tendencies evolve once we're participating in face-to-face events again.

Here are some common delivery methods that are very effective:

- **Instructor-Led, In-Person Training**: The instructor stands up in front of a room and facilitates a learning experience where learners complete hands-on or role-play exercises to demonstrate their learned skill.
- **Virtual Instructor-Led Training**: The Instructor facilitates a learning experience using a virtual meeting tool, and asks learners to toggle to join a breakout session or use another application to practice and demonstrate a particular skill.
- **Train-the-Trainer**: The instructional designer or primary facilitator teaches a group of training facilitators, local subject matter experts, or champions so they can then facilitate training or coaching with their individual work teams. We allow our instructor participants to participate as learners to familiarize themselves with the curriculum and then ask them to demonstrate their abilities by facilitating a portion of the class. While the Train-the-Trainer is not a delivery method itself, it is a method by which we enable other instructors to facilitate the instructor led courses we develop.
- **Self-Paced E-Learning**: The instructional designer creates a self-paced learning solution using an authoring tool like Captivate, Articulate, or Camtasia. There is a full continuum of quality and engagement, but those that incorporate an experiential tell-show-do approach tend to be most effective because they allow the learner to practice and demonstrate their skill.
- **Micro-learning**: The instructional designer or subject matter expert creates short subject learning using quick, easy-to-read documents with impactful images, or short-subject video recordings. Video and PDF job aids

are good examples and should take under 10 minutes for the learner to complete. Micro-learning usually addresses the "tell" and "show" parts of the learning experience but rarely provide the opportunity for the learner to "do." Still, these are great for reinforcement and very easy and inexpensive for subject matter experts to create.

- **Self-Paced Multimedia Learning Journey**: The instructional designers create a blended learning journey that employs a combination of methods, including reading, self-paced e-learning or mobile learning, videos and/or online quizzes. There may also be in-person or virtual instructor-led options, and the journey may occur over a period of weeks or even months so that it is broken down into smaller digestible chunks.

Keep in mind that if you're rolling out to a very large community of learners, your best bet may be to offer multiple methods to effectively address the highest number of learning preferences and profiles. You can build proficiency faster by reinforcing concepts using a variety of approaches. Perhaps you even use your communication plan to introduce or link to different learning opportunities throughout the weeks leading up to the actual launch as kind of a drip campaign, building on complexity and building proficiency one step at a time.

Depending on the delivery methods you choose, you may have some of the following as training deliverables or products once development is complete. These are some of the training products I've seen delivered that effectively build or reinforce learner capability:

- PowerPoint presentations, often with leader's notes to accompany training or sneak previews
- User manuals with step-by-step work instruction and screen images
- Participant guides with relevant business scenarios to use as hands-on workshops
- Job aids for quick reminders and reinforcement
- SharePoint sites or knowledge portals to serve as a central repository for learning aids
- Training scenarios and/or data (if applicable) for use in simulated learning environments
- e-learning modules with simulations posted to an LMS to track completion whenever possible
- Mobile learning solutions or apps
- Defined learning journeys, often gamified for personal best or competitive engagement
- Short subject micro-learning videos or podcasts
- Step-by-step prompts or customized help text for in-technology solution support

Developing an entirely new curriculum takes time to do, and developing effective and engaging e-learning takes even more time to do, so start your analysis as early as you can. There are pros and cons to all approaches but taking the necessary time to analyze, design, develop, implement, and evaluate effective training will expedite your organization's path to proficiency, demonstrate to your learning community that you care about their experience, and help you to achieve your desired outcomes more quickly.

IMPLEMENTATION

The implementation step in the ADDIE model is similar to the testing we discussed in our last chapter. This is not to be confused with the actual launch, which is when we actually roll out our fine-tuned training product(s) to the larger group. In the Instructional Systems Design model, we analyze, design, develop, and then implement or teach a pilot group (or two or three), so we can evaluate the effectiveness of the program and make adjustments before we offer it to the masses. Implementation is merely the act of "trying on" the training so we can observe, tweak, and improve before fully launching.

During the implementation stage, we test out each of our training deliverables, load them into our LMS (if applicable) or link them to some sort of website tracking to track completion. If applicable, we would test in-app help text or gamified solutions. We would also ensure that we have our after-class surveys and assessments in place and ready to test so we can have a thorough evaluation of the whole learning package.

When implementing training that serves technical solutions, I highly recommend aligning an early training pilot to coincide with UAT. This will raise the quality of your training because you have a captive audience of new users that will be very happy to give you critical feedback. It will raise the quality of your testing because your learners will have a scenario-based, trained level of proficiency when they're completing the testing, which will help them more critically evaluate the technical solution. Aligning the training pilot and UAT can be a challenge because it requires instructional resources to build training before the technology product is finalized. But it can be done by establishing the expectations that the training is not yet final. Observing this training in action provides valuable feedback because it allows you to observe your learners establishing the capability you wish you see in real time.

When implementing nontechnical training, it is just as important to try out learning solutions before you widely implement them. This will give you the opportunity to anticipate questions or comments, prepare responses in the form of frequently asked questions (FAQs) for use by leaders, stakeholders, and champions, and fine-tune training scenarios, so they are the most relevant to the users. Take your facilitated activities, assessments, exercises, discussion points, and case studies for a small group test drive and observe how your learners are interacting with and reacting to your training materials.

EVALUATION

Last stop! E is for **Evaluation**. I mentioned evaluation briefly in the last section, and it merely means gaining feedback so we can incorporate any changes to improve the training product(s) we deliver to build capability and support our change. We typically evaluate the effectiveness of training in a few ways:

- **After-class surveys**: Asking people to self-report their own confidence or proficiency and satisfaction with the training program and delivery.
- **Skill check assessments**: Asking people to answer questions about their newfound capabilities to evaluate whether or not they understood the intent and are able to achieve the learning objectives.

- **Skill demonstrations**: Asking people to demonstrate a newfound skill after class using technical simulations, role-play simulations, or simulation using prepared scenarios.
- **Open-ended questions**: Asking open-ended questions when you debrief certain scenarios, parts of the training, objectives or test questions will help you get thoughtful feedback with a bit of emotion from your learners. If you ask learners "How did you like it?" you're probably going to get a not-at-all-helpful "It was good!" If you ask learners to rank their confidence in a particular area, facilitate a round-robin discussion and ask them to tell you about their favorite part, challenge them to tell you what part they struggled with, or ask them to tell you what part was least engaging, you'll get much better feedback. Don't be afraid to dig in and ask for the hard feedback—that's what makes your product better.

Most importantly, the evaluation of your training objectives should align with the visionary objectives you've set out to achieve. My favorite evaluation question on a training survey is to ask the learner to evaluate on a scale of one to five how confident they are in their abilities. This evaluation step is a perfect opportunity to go back to the initial vision and ensure that the capability you're building is well aligned and is, in fact, achieving the intended outcome.

Shoestring Budget?

If you're thinking, "Tricia, this all sounds like big budget kind of stuff. We don't have an LMS, we don't have the ability to aggregate our training effectiveness…my onboarding experience was miserable! What suggestions do you have for organizations like ours that haven't yet invested in establishing performance management objectives for our individual team members? Having aligned and professional training seems like such a stretch."

Not to worry! As I said when we were discussing performance management systems for individual contributors, there's no time like the present to start, and a sizeable change initiative is a great reason to do so! Also, good training doesn't need to be extremely expensive training. It doesn't need to be perfect or shiny, either! We're all subject matter experts in one way or another, and we have technology on our side that can help us deliver great training even on a budget.

Training, much to my chagrin, has often been the lowest budget part of a project. Don't get me wrong…I'm not suggesting that it *shouldn't* have a smaller budget in comparison to other workstreams, but the technology development budget often seems to be significant in comparison to what is allocated for change management.

I do hope that this book is underscoring that we get what we pay for when it comes to change leadership and training, and often the shoestring nature of our budgets results in even more costly delays in achieving outcomes. That said, we change management professionals have done some very good work on very small budgets, and technology advancement has had a huge impact on our abilities to develop engaging training. You and your subject matter experts can do a whole lot with PowerPoint, Excel, Survey Monkey, Google Docs and Forms, YouTube, Zoom, MS Teams, WebEx and other virtual recording options.

CONVENIENT TECHNOLOGY + LEARNING MINDSET = LIFELONG LEARNING

The journey I've had in my instructional career has been so cool! When I started, we didn't have very many ways of teaching things because our tools were pretty limited.

The onus for providing training was also very much on the employer. People worked for companies sometimes for their entire careers, and it was the responsibility of the employer to promote continued employee growth by providing training. Now, not only have our technical capabilities changed for driving and delivering learning initiatives, but so have our mindsets. The onus for learning is shifting—learning is everywhere we have something to offer as a subject matter expert. How great!

Technology has enabled many of the people we have on our teams to maintain a momentum of continuous growth in their abilities. For many, it has driven a commitment to lifelong learning. People gain credentials, maintain them, and often take classes just because they're interested in continued growth and staying at the top of their game. Many have advanced degrees, and still, others are taking advantage of the non-credentialed, ongoing learning offered by educational institutions just because they can. Now, if we're stuck and need to know how to do something, we just Google it or look it up on YouTube. I can personally attest to being better read in recent years than at any point in my career because I love Audible. Prior to the pandemic, I traveled extensively, and it was always much easier to carry a book in my Audible library so I could tune out on a plane or stay alert while driving the final stretch to my destination.

Gone are the days that we have to force people to sit through hours of boring training just so we can say they did it. Now, we can let people know that they will be accountable for gaining the new skill(s) and ask them to demonstrate that they have achieved the new capability. We can still build and offer relevant training, but perhaps the expectation should be that our employees can demonstrate their capability, not prove that they've attended hours of training. Of course, it does still depend on the stakes. I think I'd rather have my brain surgeon or airplane pilot attend the required training *and* demonstrate a capability to a high degree of ongoing maturity—but in most cases, it's the successful achievement of the capability that results in the desired outcome.

A STORY

One of my favorite recent examples of building capability using this methodology and using multiple delivery methods was working with a manufacturer of low-speed vehicles. The manufacturer sold directly as well as indirectly through a large network of dealers. The company had a wide range of markets; some were growing, and some were transforming. They were exploring strategies that would allow their focus, over a period of years, to expand from a recreational use model to a commercial one. They were going to fully exploit technology to gain insight into their customers and prospects, develop a longer-term, adaptable marketing strategy, and grow a customer base.

This company had a long history in their community, a whole lot of loyalty between team members, and aligned, visionary leaders over both operations and technology. They had a service-minded group that was extremely focused on their customers' experience. This service-minded group played a product owner role in developing and evolving a technology solution that, in the

BUILDING CAPABILITY

end, served their community very well and helped them exceed their desired outcomes related to growing their new markets.

The company enjoyed brand loyalty and a general pride among the learner communities. There was strong leadership at all levels of the organization, and it was a fun project to be a part of.

To build capability, we did several things:

1. We provided a 45-minute sneak preview of the technology prior to our user acceptance testing a couple months before our launch to provide a glimpse to our learners so they could envision themselves confidently using the system. We used PowerPoint and a live demo to guide the sneak preview and asked our business leaders to reinforce the vision we had shared much earlier in the process. The most senior leader kicked off this sneak preview and shared his very inspiring multi-year vision. We were wowed by the up-front interest and the number of participants that opted in.
2. We developed training along with the development of the solution, having training deliverables in each Agile sprint (chunk of the project, for those of you who may not be familiar with the Agile concept), so that we were able to offer solid, scenario-based training to our user acceptance testers at the same time as they started their test scripts. This served as an excellent pilot for the in-person training that was aligned with UAT. It helped our testers more skillfully navigate the testing. We used PowerPoint, live demos, a simple user guide, and some job aids to support the training.
3. Our two user guides with step-by-step instructions and screen images documented the work instruction in a

friendly manner for both internal learners and our external partners. Each was only about 80 pages long, so it had a reasonable and appropriate amount of detail and was well tested for accuracy. We asked our learners to use this as their first troubleshooting resource. These user guides provided us with the steps we needed to repurpose different training topics into a variety of different delivery methods without having to reinvent the instructional wheel. For those who asked for it, we had the guides printed and drop shipped by a local printing company to our partner learners along with a branded gift to commemorate the milestone.

4. We further piloted the training by offering virtual train-the-trainer sessions to those who would be responsible for facilitating the training sessions, and in doing so, we built a five-person training team that provided personalized training to more than 1,000 people in our first several waves. The two-part train-the-trainer sessions allowed our virtual facilitators to participate as learners first, and then participate in a group teach-back so they could practice their skills in a safe and somewhat amusing environment. All people and partner managers participated in the early sessions, too, so they could have an opportunity to offer feedback and influence the approach.

5. Because we were able to develop the training throughout the technology build, we used the UAT time period to incorporate some of the more basic concepts into three simple, convenient, self-paced, but interactive e-learning modules that we asked every learner to complete before

attending the virtual, instructor-led sessions. We monitored the completion of the training in an LMS and sent a report to managers on a weekly basis so they could encourage their teams and partners to complete the necessary training.

6. We invited learners to attend two 1.5-hour virtual training sessions. We packaged the training such that each group would experience the same content. They could choose from a variety of sessions. Again, we tracked completion to build a system of accountability.

7. Because we had five people who could practically deliver this training in their sleep after a little more than two months of training, we recorded snippets of the training into short-subject topics and posted them to a learning portal so that our learners could access reinforcement videos when they needed to. These were also later built into an onboarding plan for new team members and partners. We didn't have to rebuild content, we simply edited the content we did have and taught our facilitators how to make recordings.

In the end, more than 1,200 learners experienced this learning journey, and each had the opportunity to participate in their learning using up to eight different touchpoints. They included a sneak preview demo; three self-paced, ten-minute introductory e-learning modules and two 1.5-hour instructor-led virtual sessions. Learners who signed up for virtual training could opt-in to receiving a printed user manual and job aid that was sent with an engaging cover letter, notepad, and a branded pen that added an extra personalized touch and provided them with the ability to help themselves. Of course, we also provided the electronic version for those who preferred it. We also posted short subject videos of topics that resulted in frequent questions to our knowledge-sharing sites so people could refresh their skills when necessary. What's important to note is that this journey occurred over four months, and none of the interactions required more than a 1.5-hour commitment of any one person's time.

Does it sound expensive? Honestly—it wasn't too bad! This particular organization employed me as a change management and instructional development resource, but along the way, our strategy was to utilize and build internal expertise at every turn. We started the project in September, executed our sneak previews in late January, facilitated UAT in mid-March, executed what we called pre-learning the first week of April, and launched our two-month training schedule of virtual instructor-led sessions in late April. It was a lot of work, but by enlisting already existing communication, training, and customer support channels, we were able to build expertise in the use of the technology solution, in instructional development and training delivery, and in change management and communication planning. When it was time for the internal team to embark on their second change management cycle, they were able to support it with maturely proficient internal resources. The approach of starting first by building an in-person class complete with step-by-step work instruction allowed us to spin off additional delivery methods fairly efficiently. Using the train-the-trainer events as a pilot helped us to build an army of capable experts that are still serving that organization well today.

Instructional development is really about building and testing a training product and scaling. The more learners you serve, the greater the economies of scale and the greater the value of the overall training solutions. Once you've established the work instruction, you can repurpose the initial curriculum into self-paced e-learning, virtual classes, and micro-learning delivery methods quite effectively by leveraging already existing content. Effective training, using materials that are accurate and reliable, delivered by reputable subject matter experts, and using relevant business scenarios in a manner that is convenient and engaging will build the capability you want to see, provide a good impression of the initiative, and show learners that you value their experience.

SYMPHONY: FINALE

We started this chapter focused on how the players in our symphony orchestra might build their capabilities, and we'll end by focusing on the role of the conductor.

The orchestra's leader, the conductor, analyzes the needs of its players, may design or adapt the score, or perhaps add a musician's approach to offer a special variation. He or she will develop a framework of expected practice and group rehearsal. Ultimately the group will play the score or try it on for the first time. The leader will evaluate each rehearsal, tweak, fine-tune, and reinforce until the musicians are ready for the first performance. The musical organization may provide opportunities for each player to learn and grow individually outside of this specific performance, but the onus is on the musician for knowing what they need to do to stay at the top of their game and continue their mastery of the craft.

For your symphony, imagine having a group of people who are committed to doing what it takes to be at the top of their game,

SYMPHONY

and then consider what you need to do to serve your players the best by delivering engaging, convenient, and effective learning opportunities that help your team members gain new capabilities and enable them to grow them into maturity or mastery.

Chapter 9:

ACCOUNTABILITY AND RECOGNITION

SYMPHONY: OPENING NOTES

This is kind of fun to think about—I would say the first indicator of success related to how well a symphony orchestra performs a particular score is *the applause.* Of course, there's the intrinsic knowledge of the conductor and the players themselves about the complexity of the piece and whether or not they nailed it—but the customers they're working to serve are the concert patrons and donors. Perhaps a resounding and immediate standing ovation is a five-star metric. Or perhaps it's a measurement of how long the applause lasts. If a performance yields a short trickle of golf clapping, I guess that's a pretty good indicator that there might be a need for additional rehearsals.

I'm sure there are other metrics too, like survey results of season ticket holders and donor patrons. If an orchestra delivers enough of those five-star performances, though, it results in the most important metric, which is sold-out auditoriums, top-notch ticket sales, increases in donations, endowment fund balance growth, and perhaps the ability to spread the financial love to support other musical programs.

DON'T LET UP YET!

I'm going to ask you to recall a time when you felt like some sort of a change had been rolled out with excitement and fanfare and then just dropped like a hot potato...or actually more like a mic. This happens a little too often, partly because the senior-most visionary leaders and project team resources are very engaged in the early planning stages, and by the time the group actually gets to the point where they have built an early trained level of proficiency, the leadership and project teams are moving on to the next important thing.

I can recall several times when I've asked people to recall what went well and not-so-well about the implementation of a change, and one of the responses I hear is that it came on quickly, training was like drinking from a fire hose, and then all of the support resources just moved on. It makes sense, too, because at a certain point, the heavy lifting related to planning, communicating, testing, building, and training is all behind us, and the allocation of resources and expenses begins to taper. The bummer of it is that when the leadership and resource attention begin to taper, so does the energy of the community. It would be like getting to the crescendo in the last movement of your symphony and then have the conductor place his or her baton gently on the podium. You're right there! The energy fills the room! You're ready for the

ACCOUNTABILITY AND RECOGNITION

big finish! Everyone is feeling the power of all of the instruments together at that peak. And then an unintended taper of confusion ensues and breaks the delightful momentum.

The last two elements of our change management cycle help us to ensure that continuity so we can fully realize, measure, and celebrate our achievements, build engagement, and improve.

Building a system of accountability is all about aligning appropriate metrics and sharing progress (or lack of progress) with those who can do something about it. Whenever possible, you'll want to measure both individual contribution *and* team outcomes. Measuring individual contributions raises awareness around how people are performing relative to both a performance expectation and to their other team members. Measuring team outcomes helps us to see how we're achieving as a combined team. Metrics should be nicely aligned to the visionary desired outcomes that were articulated at the onset of the change initiative. They should be simple to understand so members of your change community can easily identify with progress.

A Little Transparency Goes A Long Way

To explain this concept in its simplest form, I'm going to tell you a story of one of my earliest and more memorable change management experiences as a leader. Some time ago, back when technology and reporting capability was nowhere near as much fun as it is today, I was leading a team that was responsible for receiving and coding the weekly instructions for a mainframe transactional update process. This was a company that was responsible for managing the customer information, billing, renewal, and order processing for magazine subscriptions before so much reading was done online. Our team was responsible for managing the data files for 120 publications and tens of millions of subscribers. At the time, changes were applied as transactions to a "mainfile" during what was usually a weekly, but sometimes bi-weekly or even nightly main-file update process.

The update process meant that we would use the output file from the last update as the input mainfile, apply any new customer transactions like payments, new orders, renewal orders, changes of address, and updates to demographic data, and then produce a new output mainfile. Yes, when you think of this today, this process might resemble the technological equivalent of a stone and chisel... but at the time it was bleeding edge.

After the update completed, we would review accompanying reports and double-check numbers to be sure that all that went in was accounted for. We would create print files so we could produce paper-based billing notices, renewal notices, magazine labels, and other types of customer correspondence. We would also test different types of notices and messaging to see what yielded a higher response percentage and therefore resulted in more revenue for the publication. This was circulation marketing in the '90s. Wow! How technology has changed in the last twenty-five years.

As one might imagine, the update process didn't always progress perfectly, and we often had to do things over. We called this rework. Rework was expensive, because we often started printing things right after the update completed, so in some cases, we had to throw printed work away because it was wrong. Rework also resulted in dissatisfied customers because they had delays in the availability of their reporting. From an internal perspective,

ACCOUNTABILITY AND RECOGNITION

redoing the update meant that we had to spend valuable human and data center processing time.

When I took over the team, we had an average of 33% rework and some very unhappy customers and leaders. The team wasn't particularly happy about it either since they were doing a third of their work over again. We had a vision and an objective to significantly reduce our rework. Our initial goal was to reduce it and hold it to what we felt was a tolerable 10%.

I started capturing information about each and every rework. What was the publication? Who was the publisher? Who was the account manager? Who did the data processing instruction coding? How frequently did the publication update? What was the primary reason for the rework? I took each of these attributes and aggregated them in a spreadsheet (yes, we did have spreadsheets) so we could collectively see some trends. Weekly and monthly, I prepared simple charts that showed rework by publication, publisher, account team, coder, and primary reason.

I captured the information every day and was intentional about providing people's names at every step of the process so we could slice and dice the data by all of the different attributes if we needed to drill down. We talked about rework for a few minutes in every one of our team and client meetings, which heightened the awareness of how much rework we were doing. This was our way of reporting on individual contributions.

Simply by aggregating and publicizing the rework data, within a month, we cut our rework in half. We reached our 10% goal within a couple of months partially because the responsibility for rework became very obvious and public. Even back with the rudimentary spreadsheets we used to tally and then print our results, this was an easy-to-do and very high-impact activity. The reporting was simple, it was transparent, and it drove both personal and team ownership. Of course, we celebrated our collective achievement of the goal, and we also never stopped reporting on the rework. The continuity helped us to maintain visibility and ensure ongoing accountability for the quality expectation. It was an eye-opening experience for me because it happened so quickly, and achieving the outcome required so little effort. It was simply the act of creating collective accountability for quality through transparency and measurement.

Today, we have so many better ways to capture simple metrics that we can use to celebrate our accomplishments and provide continued awareness.

I've used and implemented Salesforce for years and love building simple reports and dashboards so people can see real-time progress on personal, team, and organizational levels. Excel Charts and Pivot Tables, Tableau Dashboard Components, Google Spreadsheets and Forms... all of these make reporting so accessible—and to us reporting and organizational development geeks, fun too!

Measuring the outcome and celebrating the team's accomplishment is the best part. Why would we not want to put some effort around continuing the recognition until we not only achieve, but exceed our goals?

The keys to creating accountability are:

- Keep the metrics simple, so they're easy for everyone to understand.
- Relate the measurement of actuals to an expectation.

- Relate the metrics to the vision and an overarching objective.
- Use people's names, when appropriate, along with other key attributes, and make the data easily accessible for all to view.
- Don't try to achieve too much all at once.

IMPLEMENTING A CRM AND PIPELINE MANAGEMENT SOLUTION FOR A SALES TEAM

Not long ago, I was doing change management discovery work for a company that was implementing CRM and pipeline management for their direct and partner sales teams. Salespeople often tell me they're well organized, know who their customers are, who their contacts are, and when they're meeting next. It's all conveniently available to them on their phones. During the discovery, we were jumping into the motivating factors, and I asked one of the leaders to tell me about how their team members were handling knowledge transfer when there was turnover in sales.

This customer's industry was going through some generational turnover (a bunch of people were retiring), and one of their pain points was the desire to have a solid history of their customer relationships so they could facilitate a more effective knowledge transfer. The leader told me the story of a guy, retiring after thirty-five years of selling, who handed him a single sheet of paper with two sides of written notes that served as his knowledge transfer on the key customers he had been serving. I think we can agree that this is a pretty seriously painful point.

Let's translate that pain into two measurable goals. Perhaps we've decided that we're going to implement a new CRM solution that will help us to gain insight into our high-revenue customers so we can understand how to serve them better and expand our relationships. One of our goals is to ask those responsible for managing relationships to capture simple data for twenty-five questions that are most important to providing insight into our relationships and continuity of business. Our billing systems show us that we have 300 key customers, an average of ten high-revenue customers per key account manager. We want 100% of the insight attributes captured for each of those 300 customers. Doable, right? If each account manager answers the questions for one key customer per day over a two-week period, we will reach our goal.

We're going to focus on achieving this early metric first for three reasons.

1. It will help us achieve a collective goal very quickly so we can have something to celebrate early.
2. It will give all of our account managers a reasonable but repetitive task right out of the chutes so they can build proficiency using the new tool.
3. It will give us the ability to aggregate and gain customer insights that demonstrate the power of the tool to our user community within the first couple of weeks, which will begin to build engagement.

We can easily provide visual management of the collective metric by providing a single bar chart with an X axis of percentage of insight attributes completed. The Y axis is the number of

ACCOUNTABILITY AND RECOGNITION

customers. We could include a sum total of all of the customers we've entered and a footer that says that our goal is 300 customers with 100% attribution. The simple graph below, at a glance, shows our progress, and requires very little explanation in showing us that our team is making progress collectively but still has some work to do.

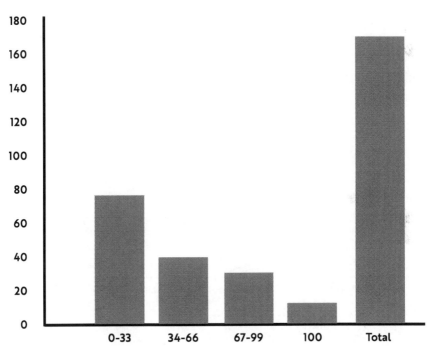

Group achieved 164/300 customers added with 16/300 at 100% attribution

If we wanted to include an individualized component, we could do a stacked bar chart that shows us, by account manager, the number of customers that had been entered, bucketed by a percentage of completion. If you were Victor looking at the graph below, what might you be thinking? We can certainly give Takisha a high five, though, right? The reality is that by making this sort of data transparent, we don't even need to have those conversations as leaders. The graphs are simple, people know where they stand relative to both the goal and to others, and with some encouragement, the team will self-correct.

CUSTOMER ENTRIES BY ACCOUNT MANAGER

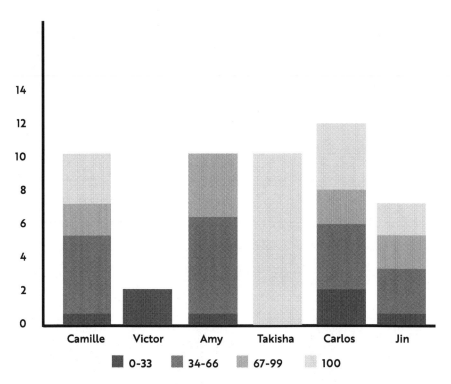

These examples are super simple measurements for tracking the entry and completeness of customer information for the purpose of improving the customer and account manager experience during transitions. Once this goal is accomplished,

ACCOUNTABILITY AND RECOGNITION

however, the curiosity sparked by the data itself is going to drive the evolution of next-generation goals and metrics. Maybe next iteration, you'll want a different goal that may be served by different data, like achieving a certain percentage increase in revenue performance despite account manager transition. Or perhaps you might aggregate and compare the overall customer satisfaction survey score from year to year for transitioned accounts. Just like iterative change cycles, we gain maturity in our metrics, and our insights become juicier with the completion of each cycle. The measurement and driving of accountability are where we start seeing accomplishment and begin to imagine new possibilities. What a bummer it would be if we were to taper our efforts before we really got to the good stuff.

Now let's look at how sharing these results impacts motivation. At first, the team might be grieving the loss of being able to manage their customer data using whatever combination of smartphone apps they discovered on their own. Most will have been on the receiving end of a crappy knowledge transfer, though, and will be able to see the business and personal benefits of capturing customer data in a consistent way. Yes, data entry sucks, but the exercise could be valuable and might even help the team to uncover some new opportunities that can beef up pipelines.

When you do the work to measure the intended outcome and can show at a glance where the team is in relationship to its goals both collectively and individually, it can really underscore the power of what you're trying to do. You can watch your charts fill up like United Way thermometers during the holiday season. And once you have that insight data captured, curiosity will lead all to want to further slice and dice that data to identify trends and target opportunities and strategies for how to maximize relationships and growth. At the very least, people will be interested in knowing that they contributed to the capture of information that is leading to some data-driven decisions and actions.

What would happen if account managers could have access to a single dashboard that showed them how many of their customers were falling behind in revenue growth, which customers hadn't had a face-to-face visit in the last four months, an exception report of any customers with less-than-delighted customer satisfaction scores, a list of all of their customers that had product deliveries or service activities in the last week so they could follow-up, and an at-a-glance view of your pipeline health? Suddenly, this is no longer an exercise in data entry or a tool for big brother to be watching…it is an assistant. A productivity tool!

Measuring our success and transparently sharing the results is a huge motivator, especially if you're ready to go with some simple metrics right out of the chutes. For those members of our community that were grieving the loss of their spiral-bound notebooks, suddenly they're a little more impressed with their leaders. Trust turns into realization. And maybe they're experiencing a teensy bit of intrinsic motivation by having contributed to something that is making a meaningful difference. Now, instead of hanging on to the inconsistent habits of the past, they begin to envision the possibilities of the future. This kind of epiphany is called *engagement*.

After completing the initial implementation, you can also begin to measure the quarterly and annual impact of a new system. I worked with an organization that measured the year-over-year sales productivity of product divisions that had implemented new sales enablement activities in relationship to those that had not yet embarked on a similar change.

Because we used the same annual measurement, we were able to compare it to a benchmark. The metrics showed a clear separation in revenue generated by salesperson for those divisions that had been a part of the sales enablement initiative in comparison to those who had not. Again, this sort of metric underscores the credibility of the decision and shows team members that the change benefitted both the organization as well as the individual. This is a definite measure of "what's in it for me?"

100 PERCENT OF TWO

We've addressed the importance of having simple, aligned, and relevant metrics and making them available for all to see, but we haven't yet discussed the importance of not trying to accomplish too much all at once. This concept is particularly important to remember for initial implementations or for the earliest change cycle. Remember back to Joe and the time sheet when we were talking about aligning appropriate rewards for performance and consequences for non-performance? When we ask people to do too much at once, we unwittingly create a punishment for good performance. Biting off and measuring a little at a time generally yields a better result in the long run because it helps us to focus collective energy.

To illustrate this using the CRM example we just discussed, let's say we were to implement the new solution, and ask people to begin:

- Managing incoming prospects

- Capturing key customers and completing the customer insights section
- Linking contact and partner information for key customers
- Entering new sales data to form a pipeline
- Capturing after-visit notes any time we have a sales interaction
- Capturing scheduled sales events in a calendar
- Linking any important email interaction to key customers and contacts

Using the list above, we're asking people to do seven new things. We can incorporate appropriate metrics to measure success, and when we do, we're going to achieve about 10% of all seven goals. We're going to achieve 100% of *none* of them. Each person is going to gravitate to the task that speaks loudest to them, and some may be more interesting than others, but as a collective, we won't have fully achieved *any* of the goals. We can keep measuring, sharing, coaching, nudging, rinsing, and repeating. We *will* continue to move the dial a little at a time. It will be quite some time, though, until we have achieved anywhere near 100% of all of the goals, which means it will be a while before we have something to celebrate.

What if, however, we clustered these new tasks and chose to focus on one or two things at a time? For example, what if in the first two weeks we simply asked people to:

- Capture key customers and complete the customer insights section
- Link contact and partner information related to the key customers

We could reasonably expect to achieve 100% or at least 90% of those first two goals within a two-week period. They're focused, attainable, measurable, and celebrate-able! We can gain some quick wins, actionable insights, a bit of engagement—and then move on to the next one or two or three. Clustering these goals in smaller chunks allows us to focus on one to three related things at a time. This means that in six to eight weeks, we will have built all sorts of proficiency and achieved much closer to 100% of *all* of our goals rather than continuing to slowly chip away.

IMPLEMENTING A NEW CALL CENTER SOLUTION FOR A CUSTOMER SERVICE TEAM

Implementing new systems that replace functionality is typically a little easier from a change management perspective. A good example of this is replacing a call center solution. You still have to push uphill before you get to the tipping point, but the hill isn't quite as steep. People are not challenging internally whether they need to have a system at all but are more interested in how the new system might be better or worse than the incumbent. People gain loyalty to systems that have served them well for years. They have built their own rapport with these systems, and believe it or not, some people have to grieve the departure of even antiquated systems as if they're saying goodbye to an old friend that they've been through some tough times with.

In the case of a service organization, we might use metrics at first to show basic adoption statistics like call productivity. In the early cycle, we might simply compare how new system productivity compares to the benchmarked productivity on the old system using average case turnaround time, cases per hour, performance in relationship to customer service level agreements, and overall post-call customer survey results. It is typical to have a dip in productivity when introducing a new system because users are not quite as proficient, but simply measuring and publishing the metrics for both team and individual performance will challenge the team to quickly return to pre-change norms.

The engagement comes, though, when we exceed those pre-change norms, and introduce new bells and whistles that help us more efficiently and effectively respond to our customers. When we show that, in fact, the new system is doing for us what we wanted it to do and we're achieving our goals.

Maybe the goal is to replace a customer service call center solution so we can take advantage of improved call scripting and access to relevant knowledge to more efficiently and completely serve our customers. We might measure this by evaluating and increasing the number of issues that our customer service agents are able to resolve in one call. I call this the one-call-close. Perhaps we also want to introduce a customer service call center solution that enables a customer portal and the ability for customers to self-serve entirely using a wizard-based questioning process.

We can provide typical customer service agent metrics such as average number of cases per hour/day, average length of inquiry or interaction by submission method, how each rep is comparing in relationship to the larger team average, and perhaps an aggregated average of their post-call survey results. To align this with the goals, however, we would need to report on what percentage of calls customers reported as being resolved in a single call and, ideally, relate it to a previous benchmark. We might also report on the number of cases resolved using a wizard-based process made available on the customer self-service portal.

Numbers talk. Being transparent about how we're doing in relationship to our goals not only challenges and focuses our teams to achieve them, but it validates our vision, shows our teams that we're collectively accomplishing what we set out to accomplish, and builds a feeling of being a part of a meaningful endeavor.

Demonstrating for a team how their work has achieved an intended outcome not only allows them to say goodbye to the old but encourages people to imagine the possibilities for what can be next.

MEASURING A CULTURE CHANGE

I don't want to say that measuring the outcomes related to a technology implementation is easy—but in comparison to measuring softer outcomes, like culture or mindset changes—it definitely is. Technology implementations are pretty black and white, and being able to provide some sort of objective metrics or key performance indicators that help team members understand their own contributions are typically part of a technology package. They're quantitative and objective. The hardest parts are making sure that you have the data you need captured so that you can truly have an aligned measurement, keeping your metrics to just a simple and digestible few, and being disciplined enough to share the results along with insight gains with some regularity.

We can still measure progress toward a culture or mindset change, though, and it may be even more important to do so to build and maintain ongoing momentum. Culture changes differ because they take a lot longer to authentically achieve. If you're looking to change a culture or a mindset, you might as well nestle in, prepare to be patient, and maybe even do a little continuity planning.

If I were to return to the example of the culture change initiative at the subscription fulfillment company after we had been purchased as sort of a corporate fix and flip, we would have had several types of measurements. If I had to do it today, I would have a monthly quantitative report of activities, maybe in the form of a newsletter. How many culture workshops have been held? What were the averages or outcomes of the post-workshop survey questions? How many people have been touched by a workshop in relation to our goals? I would also include anecdotal stories and highlights of both positive comments and lessons learned. Calling out certain regions or teams specifically would also help to personalize the report so that people could relate individually to having participated in one of the events. Helping people to recall the positive feelings evoked at a particular interaction helps to keep the initiative top of mind and remind them of their contributions to a meaningful goal.

The other way I might have reported information would be to move the dial on the overall goal. In the example, the culture change was done in response to an employee satisfaction survey question that had taken a significant dip. We had a benchmark. To tie the measurement back to the goal, we would need to compare the year-over-year results of the employee satisfaction survey question that represented the driver of the change. In this case, since it was an annual survey, it would have required some patience.

That said, we can get some leading indicators by capturing some initiative-related data. While I don't like over-surveying, I do like including super simple polling (like three questions) executed quarterly or twice annually. Something like, "On a scale of one to five, with five indicating very high impact, how impactful do you think our culture initiatives have been to date?

Perhaps we could break this down into facilitated events, ongoing living the values messaging, and discussions with work team members. The results from these types of surveys will give you some data, albeit subjective, and some indication of whether your efforts are leading to the improvement you seek. One of my favorite newer ways to survey is the use of those smiley face buttons. Have you ever been in a public restroom where there was a stand placed right at the exit with two buttons—a green happy face and a red frown face? It's pretty easy to hit the button on the way out. It's easy to provide the data, is a low barrier for the facility user, and a pretty straightforward metric for measuring the cleanliness of a public restroom. You find it either acceptable or not.

Now there are technical solutions available that allow us to send an email equivalent of the smiley face buttons to ask for simple feedback. Something like this, used somewhat sparingly, would be great for polling a culture initiative. It is a low barrier, builds active rapport, gives us a valuable metric, and provides us with honest data that we can share with the larger team to help show progress.

RECOGNIZING RESULTS

Metrics are powerful, and results absolutely drive engagement and excitement. It would be so great to think that you're always positively moving toward your goal and celebrating success. The truth is that sometimes that's not the case…and sharing results with the team always needs to be authentic and transparent. If results are ugly, we can address them with constructive commentary and with public encouragement. I use the four-to-one rule whenever possible, whether I'm delivering improvement feedback individually or to a larger group. The four-to-one rule simply says that, whenever possible, we call out four positive pieces of feedback in relation to one piece of improvement feedback.

Let's say we encouraged our sales team to enter those 300 customers, and after a week, we had only twenty-five. First, I would check my metric to be sure the numbers were accurate. Then, if validated, I would absolutely share the dismal results, and paint them red. I might call out the work and IT resources for having delivered an easy-to-use questionnaire, I might thank the person who pulled together the report, I might call out the one person's excellent performance for having added ten customers with complete attribution, and I might make an honorable mention of any of the other team members who had at least made an effort. Then I would ask for people's renewed commitment and restate my expectation that we would have 300 completed customers entered by the end of week two. If this were a much larger group, I would also check in with my representative champions to get their insights into why we were missing the mark.

This takes us all the way back to Joe and the time sheet. Simply restating our expectations and asking the question, "Why didn't you do it?" is often all you need to create accountability and drive your outcome. This is what we mean by pushing uphill. We ask, share results, address what we can, continue to nudge, and just keep repeating and doing the work until we get to the top of the hill—the tipping point. Once we get there, momentum takes hold, and we can enjoy the ride.

There is an appropriate escalation here, though. We start with proactive communication, publicly share results, issue friendly reminders, ask the group "why not?" and then host individual conversations with those who are not coming along with the rest of the group. We stay the course and repeat until we get to the top of the hill. Stick to your vision and expectation, though! You'll get there faster by standing firm.

SENIOR STAKEHOLDER SUPPORT

Remember when we were talking about when to enlist the support of your most senior-level stakeholders?

We said that it was appropriate to do so when it is time to communicate your vision because you want your senior-most stakeholder to lead the charge. The next time to enlist the support of that person is not long after you've begun to report your first results. Asking that senior leader to comment on the results one way or another will reinforce the already positive contributions, or, if necessary, create accountability by letting people know that the senior leader is paying close attention.

When I'm working on a change initiative, I like to spend some time showing our senior stakeholders how to find metrics in relation to our outcomes, highlight excellent performance, and share where we have an opportunity to improve. Sometimes I'll encourage those senior leaders to personally email a few people to thank them for their excellent attention or ask a detailed question about something they learned that is related to the change. It's a good idea for the leader to copy the person's manager on any messages, not only to keep them in the loop but also to spread positivity.

Word travels fast, and when the word gets out that the Senior VP, the CEO, or even a community leader is paying attention to the metrics and reaching out to individual contributors, it definitely drives both accountability and the feeling of accomplishment. Easy to do, high impact!

SYMPHONY: FINALE

If I were to try to put myself in the shoes of a musician, the applause is going to give me immediate feedback, which is pretty much the epitome of a Key Performance Indicator (KPI), right? Knowing I'm part of a high-performing team of musicians that deliver unparalleled performances over and over again to support a world-renowned orchestra that is able to spread its support to other municipal arts programs is even more impactful, and may be part of a larger vision for a metropolitan symphony. Whether it is the conductor or perhaps some other leader of a performing arts council, sharing the results related to the impact a symphony orchestra's overall contributions are having on a particular program, season, or even community is an even more powerful intrinsic motivator for the many of the individual players who make up the orchestral team.

Chapter 10:

ITERATE AND IMPROVE

SYMPHONY: OPENING NOTES

We've come full circle with our Symphony. We planned our season's performance up front and filled our stage with talented musicians. We communicated our inspiring vision for what we wanted to accomplish in the season. We took care of our musicians and nurtured them by offering access to excellent equipment, facilities, and training. We built capability through individual practice and tried out our full performances through collective rehearsals. We measured our own reactions, incorporated feedback from our peers, coaches, and conductor, and then we practiced and rehearsed some more. We dotted our i's and crossed our t's. We delivered our first live performances to our patrons, and we measured our success by applause. Ticket sales are strong, we're exceeding our donor goals, and we are able to spread our good fortune to others. Now, with each and every performance, we'll continue to improve, and we'll embark on a regular cadence of introducing new scores and new focus so that we can continue the momentum and perform to our highest standard.

GROW FROM PROFICIENCY TO ENGAGEMENT

Yes! We've reached the end of our change management cycle. We're continuing to support our people as they mature in their capability and evolve into their new sense of normal. We're building engagement and awareness because we're measuring our results, sharing our progress, and recognizing contributions. We're targeting our problem areas and soliciting ideas and feedback from our entire change community. Last stop…don't stop! Continue to grow your engagement through ongoing iteration and improvement.

Remember much earlier in the book when I was talking about the sciences organization with 1,200 salespeople, who had an average tenure of seventeen years? We were discussing loyalty as a motivating factor, and I talked about the lovely gentleman, just a couple of years from retirement, who thanked me for his training materials because while he wasn't much into new technology, he was going to ask his son for help, and he was going to be sure his work got done. For this chapter, I'm going to fast-forward with that memorable customer because they were an excellent example of iterating and improving.

The initial implementation cycle for that customer was about a year. The care team, made up of five full-time people, measured, supported, and continued to nurture this organization of salespeople until they exceeded their goals. The learning curve was pretty steep, but ultimately, a couple of goals at a time, they reached the tipping point. Momentum took hold, and using this new system became the new norm. As the sales regions started to achieve results and began using their new data to gain insights that led to more strategic activities, they became engaged. They also experienced how this new solution helped them to become more productive and serve their customers better. Once they were engaged, the ideas started to flow. It was like turning on a spigot. "Wow...could we use this to (fill in the blank)?"

As would be expected, this high-functioning team with a service-minded CIO at the helm developed a system for capturing these ideas, prioritizing them, and acting on them so there could be continued improvement. This was not a one-time transactional new technology event; this was a platform that they would continue to evolve indefinitely. Ultimately, project resources like me rolled off, and even the care team members returned to their previous roles. One or two stayed behind in new roles that were responsible for the ongoing solicitation, prioritization, implementation, and communication of additional features and change cycles. Many IT organizations refer to this practice as setting up an ongoing governance that ensures excellent hand-off and continuity. Some larger organizations, especially if multiple communities are being served, will establish the concept of a Centers of Excellence (CoE) to oversee the governance and continuity. Several years later, the CIO called me. She said, "Tricia, I have some news."

Our organization was just acquired, and even though the company that we're now a part of has a different platform for CRM and sales automation, we asked to keep *our* system. We worked hard to get where we are today, and our system has evolved into a tool that is serving us so much better than we ever could have imagined, and our salespeople really, authentically like it. So we asked them, please—don't take our system away! I'm happy to say that they gave us our wish, and now we need to onboard a whole bunch of new salespeople who will be migrating to *our* system. Can you help?"

Naturally her phone call made me smile, and of course, we moved forward with onboarding the new group.

This CIO and the sales leaders who were our senior stakeholders just modeled the type of service-centric leadership and commitment to change that this is all about. They reached a symphony, or perhaps I should say they continued it.

First, they cared about how people felt and what motivated them, they had goals and desired outcomes that were well thought out and measurable, they articulated a vision that people could get behind, they nurtured an ongoing rapport, tested the heck out of that system to ensure the technology was as easy to use as possible and was ultra-aligned with the sales process. They invested in building capability, measured and recognized success, and most importantly, they solicited ideas and built the governance for iteration and ongoing improvement that helped them not only meet 80% of their goals, but to exceed their 100% goals and to move on to achieving a level of maturity they couldn't even have imagined during their initial change cycle. Because they listened and encouraged ideas, they were able to continue to improve, and in the end, the system became something their people found so valuable that they asked their acquiring company not to take it away from them. It is no wonder these people had an *average* tenure of seventeen years at a high-achieving company. I would be loyal too!

ITERATE AND IMPROVE

BUILDING RAPPORT WITH YOUR CHANGE COMMUNITY

Now that we've explored each of the elements in our change cycle, shortly we'll move on to how to build this into a more detailed change management and communication plan, complete with a simple Gantt chart timeline that you can use as a tool to manage this type of endeavor. A thread that spans the entirety of our initial change cycle and beyond is ongoing, effective communication. Not too much, not too little, but just enough friendly communication that helps people stay informed about the change effort and encourages participation by building rapport.

Rapport infers that there's a dialogue, though, right? Which means that we need to ensure, at every step of the journey, that there's an opportunity for *any* member of the community to ask a question or share a comment or an idea. Those questions, comments, and ideas should be captured in a centralized place so they're not lost.

We can acknowledge questions in the form of a FAQ list, we can call out comments in regular monthly communications or project updates, we can stimulate dialogue in team meetings by providing speaking points on leadership briefs, we can respond to requests for help by providing support, and we can capture ideas for improvement in an idea portal that can be evaluated for prioritization and action. Ultimately, as we settle into an ongoing cadence, we can reduce the burden on our community stakeholders or champions by tapering the frequency of our regular meetings. We might even re-shuffle the resources a bit to share the responsibility, but we should continue indefinitely until we collectively decide that there are no remaining priorities for the team to accomplish.

Conversely, remember the last chapter when I asked you to recall a time when you got to the end of an initiative that had lost steam as soon as the project resources and leaders had moved on to the next best thing? It felt like the initiative was dropped, and the energy escaped like the air from a deflating balloon. What do you think happens to trust, culture, motivation, and loyalty when those comments and ideas for improvement fall into that black hole of "I submitted it to someone but never heard back?" Cynicism happens. Trust, credibility, and loyalty decline. Excitement and engagement wane. And the opportunity to contribute positively to culture becomes a missed one. We risk settling into complacency and perhaps worse—settling for mediocrity.

Rapport is important. Just like when we're having a conversation with a single person, we need to treat others the way we want to be treated and acknowledge the contributions of any one of the team members who choose to take the time to submit a question, request, idea, or comment. We can do this en masse. We don't have to respond individually to every single inquiry, comment, or idea, and we may decide that some ideas aren't ones we want to implement, but we do need to acknowledge them. This is when we put on our service-minded-leader hats and remember that as change managers, project leaders, and people leaders, our *customers* are the members of our change community.

IDEAS FOR ITERATION AND IMPROVEMENT

What can you do to promote iteration and improvement for your change initiative? Here are some ideas. These aren't particularly difficult to do. Some require more resources than others, but they can be baked into a repeatable process that ensures

ITERATE AND IMPROVE

continuity and keeps the resource requirement to a minimum.

1. Begin to establish rapport early, with the first visionary message. Build a centralized email address or web form (think SharePoint or even a Google Form) where people can submit questions, comments, and ideas. Establish a regular cadence of determining the responses to questions and include the responses, only when appropriate to do so, in your messaging and communication plan.
2. Whenever possible, publish questions, answers, ideas, and status in a transparent way so people can see the activity and progress. This sort of transparency builds accountability for change leaders and governance boards to remain committed to the dialogue and taking forward-moving action. After the initial change cycles, the frequency of this type of communication can certainly taper, but it should continue throughout the life of the change initiative.
3. Work with leaders, project stakeholders, and representatives of the community to establish a simple, repeatable governance process for definition, approval, prioritization, implementation, and change management of new ideas. The governance process should include the definition of new desired outcomes that will serve as the vision element of your subsequent change cycle. This new visionary element may not require the support of the senior-most leader, but it will require visionary communication from the COE leader or product owner.
4. If your organization or initiative is extremely large scale or your change initiative will continue to evolve indefinitely,

set up a regular call cadence with a governance board that will oversee the definition and continuity of additional cycles. For technology initiatives, we often refer to these governance boards as Centers of Excellence (CoEs).

5. Commit to action. Not all ideas are going to get implemented, and it is okay to reject an idea or prioritize it lower on the list. If you're going to solicit ideas, however, plan to act and keep the ideas fresh. Make a commitment that your idea box will not turn into the proverbial one that is more synonymous with a black hole.

6. Budget and plan for ongoing cycles of innovation and change. Subsequent change cycles are typically much smaller in comparison to the budget, scope, and timeline you may have planned for in the initial change cycle. But establishing a structure and the governance for continuity will require some number of resources. Planning for continuity when establishing the initial budget will make it much more likely to occur.

ITERATE AND IMPROVE

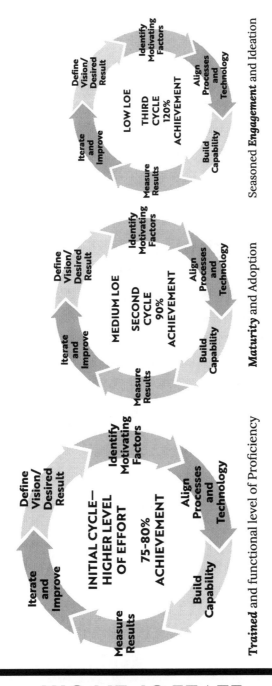

Iteration and improvement are the culmination of all the other elements. If we have done our due diligence through our discovery work, explored motivating factors, shared and solicited active participation in a vision, ensured our desired change is well aligned with our processes and technology, built capability and proficiency, measured our progress, and recognized both successes and misses all while communicating effectively and building rapport at every turn—we *will* engage people.

Engaged people who trust that their contributions will be acted upon will offer suggestions and ideas. Those suggestions and ideas evolve into additional change cycles, greater proficiency, more mature thought, and greater achievement. The continued maturity and evolution of the contributions of all of these individual players result in an organizational flow. A unified, harmonious, and often even masterful achievement.

Technology is evolving at an unprecedented rate right now. Platforms evolve, new capabilities are introduced, and there are always new problems to solve or opportunities to exploit in the most positive of ways. If we're not iterating and planning for ongoing improvement, we're missing out on some significant efficiencies to be gained and, as importantly, we're missing out on new, more streamlined ways of offering our internal and external customers the best possible experiences.

A COUPLE OF STORIES

I worked with a company not long ago that had several different divisions that all had multiple focuses, but largely within the same industry. They had their first change cycle almost five years ago, and today they serve several thousand people. Since that time, the technology platform we implemented during the first cycle has expanded significantly. There are new AI capabilities, new wizard-based questionnaires, new bot capabilities, and new, lower-cost options for connecting to other systems. Possibilities that we could not even consider five years ago are now a reality.

Happily, this company was set up to enjoy these new capabilities as they came along. They had an ongoing monthly governance process that had an evolving team of business stakeholders and a dedicated team of technical resources, which they called the CoE. They have regular meeting cadences and an established process for submitting ideas and enhancement requests, along with an established process for prioritization and action. When a new idea is bigger than a breadbox, there is also a process in place for establishing a business case and gaining funding for additional investments. As a result, stuff gets done, and iteration and improvement happen.

I talked about this company earlier, in fact, because one of its early cycles got off to a rocky start when one of the visionary leaders left just after the approval of the project and establishment of the implementation team. They did exceed their goals, but not until after quite an upstream paddle. Once they got there, though, they were committed to gaining the most they could out of the technology they chose. Last I checked, they continued to iterate, each and every month, through their ongoing governance. They had a strong business leader who absolutely believed in the technology. They made data-driven discoveries and acted on them with technology. Small bits of investment turned into tens of millions of dollars in outcomes. Today, if you were to ask one of their users how they feel about the platform, I'm sure the answer would be tepid, because people tend to take their technology solutions for granted after a while. If, however, you asked them if they would like to return to their previous solution, they would answer unequivocally, "No way!" Collectively, their organization, efficiency, productivity, and share of wallet has improved.

If this organization would have stopped after the initial implementation and not continued to iterate and improve, I believe the entire initiative would have fizzled. They had to push hard to gain momentum before they realized their goals. But once they did, it was much smoother sailing with a very favorable wind. I applaud their relentless efforts though, for pushing to get over that initial tipping point.

CHANGING A CULTURE

Let's compare and contrast this, though, to a cultural change, and then figure out how we can establish an ongoing center of excellence, governance, and cadence to help us drive iteration, improvement, or at the very least, continuity for inclusivity. Historically, I think cultural changes have been a little harder to quantify or justify a business case for, and I want to challenge us to crack this nut, because I believe we can and must.

A number of years ago, a colleague and I attended a required diversity and inclusion training for leaders. It was led by a virtual facilitator who, at one point, instructed us to join a virtual breakout session. The way people were paired up was random, and a female colleague and I found ourselves in a breakout room with another person who happened to be male. We were asked to explore a made-up scenario where a hiring manager was addressing his all-male team. He explained that while the woman he recently interviewed was certainly qualified to do the required work, he wasn't sure that a woman would be a good cultural fit for the all-male team. Our breakout task was to discuss how we might respond to this situation in an effort to be inclusive.

My colleague and I, who had both endured many years in a technology industry that very definitely favored the other gender, were honestly aghast that this still had to be a question, and we were both prepared to offer our responses. When we heard our third party's response...you could have heard a pin drop.

He said, absolutely in earnest, "I don't know. It really doesn't affect me... why would I say anything? A woman probably *wouldn't* be a good fit for our team."

Really? In the new millennium? How is this sort of answer even possible in a professional world? Diversity and inclusion are our responsibility! This world is filled with smart people! We want those smart people, and we want that diversity represented on our teams. This means our leadership teams, too! Our organizations are healthier and more creative when people are working and earning and learning and excelling. Our leadership teams need to represent the diversity of the world and of our organizations, too. If your teams lack diversity, you're missing out on so much creativity and opportunity. But yes...this happened, and it was not that long ago. The "cultural fit" excuse happens all the time. We have some work to do, everyone. This is a collective problem.

I want my white son and my grandson to have opportunity, but not at the expense of the opportunities of my very capable daughter or daughter-in-law or granddaughter, or my Black, Brown, Asian, or Indian friends. We have to fix this. We need to spread the love.

I'm hoping the example above is just an anomaly, and my colleague and I experienced the most surprising of breakout session comments. But in the interest of driving change, how do we ensure iteration and continuous improvement for inclusivity and diversity? Clearly, there is still a whole lot of privilege bestowed on a very particular set of genetic circumstances. I feel that, as a society, because this involves our employment, we often choose not to rock the boat.

More and more organizations are implementing diversity and inclusion roles, but perhaps they need to be COEs. And perhaps these COEs need to establish organizational bylaws, structure, and governance so that even after the appointed diversity and inclusion leaders depart organizations, the initiatives and related action continue. Maybe these initiatives don't have to just drop, like a thud, until some inspiring, motivated and interested party decides to pick them up again.

Women got the right to vote over one hundred years ago in the US, and men of non-white races gained that right before that. Equal opportunity laws were enacted almost a half century ago. There's no question that, as a nation, we need to up our game across the organizations we work for and around the communities we live in. On the diversity and inclusion front, we need to figure out this ongoing iteration and improvement factor for continuity because we are a long way from achieving symphony. But! Let's save that topic for another book and end on a high note.

SYMPHONY: FINALE

It's the last performance of the season. Our maestro steps up to the podium, lifts his baton, and we perform almost flawlessly.

We find that collective flow, those moments of being in the zone when time seems to stand still, that moment of seemingly effortless bliss. We soar over our peaks and dip into our valleys, moving from strings to brass to woodwinds. Percussion accompanies us at every turn. The connected energy fills the room. Every person experiences the waxing and waning power and emotion of the performance. We finally descend into a quiet pianissimo as our conductor slowly brings his finger to his lips and with a gentle movement of his hands, brings us back to silence and closure with a satisfied smile. We sit in a brief, lovely moment of quiet reflection that soon erupts with the sound of applause. It was a good night. It was a good season. We did good work.

Chapter 11:

IMAGINE THE POSSIBILITIES

WOW—WHAT A JOURNEY THIS BOOK HAS BEEN! As I write this final chapter, I am in awe of all that transpired over the course of this experience. I wish I could say the awe has been of the inspiring, positive type, but honestly, I think 2020 and 2021 will go down in history as two of the tougher years in American history.

It has been inspirational in many ways, though, and certainly motivating, because we often find out what we're made of in times like this. The entire globe has been faced with a pandemic, and many have faced widespread unemployment, economic stagnation, and civil unrest. In the United States, we've also faced rioting in response to systemic racism resulting in unequal treatment by law enforcement and unequal death rates as a result of the pandemic. As I finish this book, more than 805,000 lives have been lost to COVID 19 in the United States. This is a reality that none of us imagined two years ago, and yet here we are. On a positive note, vaccines have now been widely distributed, and we're starting to return to a new version of normal.

When I talk about motivation, consider the difference between February of 2020 when we had a very low, 3% unemployment that spiked to 14.7% in April when we all shut ourselves in to help slow the spread of this infectious virus, before falling to 7.9% again in September and then increased again around the holidays. Suddenly, many found themselves a lot less picky and a lot more grateful for their employment situations. Don't expect that motivating factor to stick indefinitely though. People have had a lot of extra time on their hands to reflect on what's important to them, and those with skills in high demand will definitely have a choice. Caring about your organization's culture and experience is as important now as it ever has been because a battle for the best talent is in full force.

Voters on both sides of the aisle would also agree that 2020 required us to endure what was perhaps the most divisive election cycle in history. The election was decided, once again, on a very narrow margin, with a whole lot of people feeling extremely passionate about their candidate. The silver lining? We've had an unprecedented number of people register to vote and exercise their right to participate in our democracy.

For me? I think there is so much that needs changing. Maybe, at the forefront, it is helping people to realize that every single one of us has a different perspective, and different perspectives are not wrong… most of them are just different. Most perspectives just need to be listened to and honored. All people want to feel heard. Democracy is absolutely about making policy that serves the majority of people. We exercise our voices by exercising our votes.

There are some things that are just wrong, too, and we need to call them out. We cannot tolerate hate, violence, child abuse, human trafficking, cruelty, or racism in society. We must step up our work as communities, organizations, and nations when it comes to combatting these things because we denounce them as members of the human race. I believe we need to step up our efforts to stamp out hateful behaviors and work to embrace our diversity as we foster inclusivity and create opportunity.

All of this requires an intentional effort to drive change at multiple levels. We can start with ourselves, our workplaces, and our communities. We don't have to wait for an act of Congress to begin to make changes in our workplaces and communities. To quote Mohandas Gandhi, we can "be the change we want to see in the world." We can be the leaders, the stakeholders, the champions, and the change managers for our own change communities.

This ugly pandemic has required us to be present in our smaller communities and act locally in ways that we may not have had to even think about before.

Whether we wanted to or not, some of us spent more time getting to know our families, neighbors, and even our children because we were shut in together for months. Some banded together as neighborhoods and families to get creative and plan outdoor, mask-wearing, socially distanced events. Many of us were just doing our best to soldier on through our boredom, depression, stir-craziness, and loneliness while staying hopeful that we would again be able to travel to exciting places, attend concerts, go to sporting events, or simply enjoy visiting fully packed restaurants or bars without worrying about the health consequences of doing so.

We do change when we're motivated to change, and this year has kicked many of us into action. My hope is that we can bottle up those silver linings, keep the goodness that has come out of these painful years, start rolling up our sleeves, and work together to drive some positive change. We can do this. We have the "how." Now let's focus on defining the "what" and get to work!

CIVIL RIGHTS AND DIVERSITY

Fostering inclusivity, appreciating diversity, and addressing systemic racism seem like a great place to start. For me, it is appalling to see what a truly poor job we've done advancing civil rights in our country. I'm not saying that nothing has been done over the last fifty years, but really? We could have done, and should have done, and can do so much more.

As any good change manager would, I dissect our history into change cycles. What was it about the 1850s that motivated the change to abolish slavery? What motivated a congress of only white men to enact the emancipation proclamation? What happened in the 1870s when a congress of white men gave black men the right to vote? What happened in the 1960s to influence action during the civil rights movement? Was it the visionary leaders and amazingly articulate and talented orators? Was it everyday violence and horror that was occurring in many cities and on campuses? Was it the continued peaceful protesting?

Whatever the catalysts, whatever the motivators, the net result is that despite some promising spikes of improvement, we have, as a nation, made excruciatingly slow progress. I always arrive at the conclusion that when we don't have clear, measurable objectives, we don't have simple or transparent metrics, people don't know what they can do to move the dial, we don't have accountability and transparency among the masses, and we don't have focused energy or continuity. We tend to have little microbursts of change and then just settle back into our complacent worlds...with mediocre or perhaps just abysmal results. I truly hope this year will serve as a catalyst for the next burst of progress.

When I was in kindergarten, I lived in Kalamazoo, Michigan. In 1973 I entered kindergarten at a time of school integration. Kids from my neighborhood were being bussed to schools in other neighborhoods, and kids from other neighborhoods were being bussed to our neighborhood school. While I went to kindergarten and first grade at my neighborhood school, my sisters were bussed to schools outside our neighborhood.

I lived in a predominantly white part of town but was lucky to have experienced a quite diverse early education experience. My teacher was black, and there was a pretty good mix of black and white kids in our classroom.

When I look back on that experience solely from the perspective of a five-year-old little girl, I'm really glad I had it. I'm sure there were all sorts of expenses and inconveniences that went along with the integration of schools, but I for one, experienced learning in a group of people that had all sorts of differences at a time when our community was making a concerted effort to celebrate and explore those differences rather than being fearful of them.

What happened? Where did it fall off? Did we not achieve the results? Were there too many barriers? Was it too expensive?

Or—did the attention wane? Did we stop measuring? Did our more visionary community leaders move on to the next most important thing? Did we stop improving? Did we lose motivation? I'm sure it was probably a combination of many of these factors. But at the end of the day, we didn't hold ourselves accountable, and we didn't have the governance, oversight, or perhaps focus in many of our communities to drive iterative continuity and ongoing action.

Halfway through first grade, my family moved to Boulder, Colorado. Boulder was, and is, the absolute opposite of diverse. I wonder what my black and brown friends think when they see Boulder being named by the US News and World Report as the best place to live in the US in the year 2020? I will agree that it is absolutely beautiful, and I still love to visit. It has a high quality of life for those who can afford to live there. But how could a kid grow up in Boulder, Colorado, and have any way to authentically empathize with the situation of a black kid being raised in the south side of Chicago or in George Floyd's Minneapolis neighborhood? We might be able to gain some insight if we choose to educate ourselves or visit, but really? Most of us, myself included, are just plain ignorant. Our intentions are probably pretty good, but we tend to stay to ourselves and hang out with our friends and family communities. The plight of others is often simply out of sight, out of mind, and the captivity of COVID-19 has made this even worse.

Still, I do believe that the nation, at least from a civil rights perspective, is probably a much better place now than it was in 1968. We are definitely a much better place now than we were in 1860 and before. Many of our communities have continued to chip away at change because change happened, and some communities did a pretty good job at planning for that continuity. But from a national perspective, we can, and should, do so much better.

- We can pass laws that require police departments to publish the metrics that show us how many people died at the hands of law enforcement year over year and month over month.
- We can build a database that helps us to break these numbers down by location, race, gender, religion, sexual orientation. And we can plot it out on an aesthetically pleasing, simple chart to benchmark our progress. In fact, I bet we already have this data.
- We can work with our visionary leaders to help us set goals and visualize what we can achieve.
- We can use technology to analyze, communicate, build rapport, and publicly recognize results.
- We can enlist the support and influence of representative members of our communities to serve as champions of our cause.
- We can establish a small number of simple, informed goals at community, regional, state, and national levels that say we're going to reduce this number by a certain percentage in a fixed amount of time.
- We can explore and identify the factors among communities and law enforcement that contribute to the fear and hate. We can choose one or two or three things at a time to focus on.
- We can create accountability, transparency, and awareness. We can recognize and celebrate progress while continuing to address our transgressions through an educated frame of reference. We can incorporate well-placed polls to keep our fingers on the pulse of the action.

- We can examine our motivating factors to explore our own personal biases and figure out why, for so many communities and people, this issue seems to be considered one that only people of color need to solve.
- We can solicit ideas for our next set of desired measurable outcomes that will become the visions for our subsequent change cycles.
- We can plan for continuity and ongoing iteration and improvement in our communities, regions, and states. We can share best practices, establish continuous improvement, focus our collective energy, and innovate.
- We can continue our change cycles, year after year, and continue our uphill push until we've reached that tipping point and can finally enjoy our momentous ride.

And, when that day comes, we can stay the course and continue our measurement and awareness for generations.

Working to Understand and Honor the Perspectives of Others

While writing this book, I found one underlying theme that recurred over and over. It is the concept that our perspectives and opinions aren't the *only* right ones. We look for the most common motivating factors and preferences when we plan our change efforts, with the understanding that our own might not be widely shared by others. People have different experiences, world views, circumstances, and living situations that shape their own understanding of the world. Our perspectives are unique! They're à la carte! They differ!

Empathy is about working to understand the experiences and perspectives of others and authentically caring about them.

Maybe, at the root of all of this change, is learning how to understand another's perspectives, finding relationship through our commonalities, and figuring out how to talk respectfully through our differences of opinion.

I'm lucky to have had the ability to travel to many other countries. It has given me the opportunity to see that a whole lot of people on this globe live quite happily in countries that are not the USA. I love the United States of America—and there are also many differently successful ways of living in the world. We live in a country with fifty very different states—we are a melting pot society made up of a majority of immigrants.

We have a multitude of races, ethnicities, and religious preferences, not to mention genders and sexual orientations. Of course, we have different world views and opinions, and the opportunity that represents is always what has made up the American dream.

In recent years we've become increasingly divided, though, I think perhaps at the root of our divisiveness is simply a lack of understanding, and perhaps a lack of interest in figuring out how we can peacefully coexist with our various perspectives. Many organizations and communities have implemented programs that encourage inclusivity and celebrate diversity and expose their members to different points of view. As a result, the ideas, accomplishments, and outcomes of those organizations and communities often thrive.

Imagine communities where people with all different perspectives prosper, experience similar access to quality childcare and education, and have access to excellent jobs and earning potential. Imagine communities where law enforcement officers with a history of violence are held accountable, and when brutality is not tolerated. Imagine a community where people who hold different opinions can discuss them in a respectful way, without fear of retaliation, and work toward common solutions for the problems they face. We can achieve this vision, or, at the very least, we can get a lot closer to it.

In closing, if you leave this book with *one single nugget*, I hope it is this:

You are the leaders of people, projects, teams, organizations, communities, and beyond. *You* influence the cultures of your groups every single day just in the way you work with them. *You* set the bar for your organizational cultures. *Your* expectations establish the continuum of what you're willing to accept as good, great, or excellent. *Your* challenge of the status quo prevents the rest of us from getting comfortable with mediocrity and demands the highest standards. *Your* willingness to be in service to your team members and intention to care about the experience they have makes an enormous difference—*and* it inspires others to do the same.

These principles of managing change require us to consider what makes people successful. They force us to consider different perspectives, and they ask us to *care* about the individual motivators of the many. They require us to take actions that minimize angst and maximize collective success, and they require us to deliver to a high standard. All of this matters, whether you're implementing a new technology solution, implementing a new process, transforming an organizational structure, improving a corporate culture, choosing your leadership team, rolling out a campaign to raise awareness of personal bias, working to transform accountability in a law enforcement community, or leading an orchestra of talented musicians who offer their patrons a season of awe-inspiring symphonic treasures.

APPENDIX PROCESS AND TOOLS

I PLACED THIS CHAPTER AT THE VERY END as an appendix to introduce some processes and tools I use to define and plan projects. I'll paint it red by saying this chapter might be a little dry unless you get excited by project plans, Gantt charts, and lists of deliverables.

I would be remiss, though, if I left you hanging, having only regaled you with stories of how the elements on the cycle work together to promote change but with no process or tools that you can use to drive your own change initiatives.

It is pretty tricky to plug detailed spreadsheets onto the printed page while still allowing them to be readable, so instead of attempting to do that, I'll introduce some suggestions here and point you to my website so you can view simple examples that may be helpful to you. My intent is to equip as many people as possible who are passionate and thoughtful about driving change with tools that can help facilitate their change journeys and influence the success of their outcomes.

HIGH-LEVEL PROCESS

We follow a repeatable process for doing all of our discovery work and planning so we can keep ourselves organized and be sure to address all of the important elements we just explored on the change cycle. The steps in our process lead to deliverables that are listed and defined in the next section. Keep in mind that no two change initiatives are the same, but we follow similar activities to arrive at the tailored approach for each community and initiative. This section lists the most repeatable activities in our process in a simple way, which, if we were to align with dates, would result in a tactical order and aesthetically pleasing Gantt chart! Of course, each of these high-level activities can be broken down further into sub-activities to reach a more granular level of detail that you may wish to achieve with a project plan.

Facilitate Discovery and Articulate Vision

- Facilitate initial discovery with colleagues, project stakeholders, and those who appear to be passionate visionaries.
- Summarize key discovery findings, and your proposed approach in a Change Management Summary.
- Validate the Change Management Summary with leaders and stakeholders initially, and with community representatives once they're engaged.
- Articulate objectives, desired outcomes, measurements, and behaviors for visualization.
- Craft initial visionary messaging and work with the senior-most leader or stakeholder to execute.
- Identify and enlist community representatives (champions).

- Establish a centralized repository for all change management summaries, plans, notes, communication, and instructional deliverables.

Establish an Ongoing Communication Plan that Addresses Motivating Factors and Builds Rapport

- Develop a high-level project and communication plan for the change management work stream, incorporating preferences and addressing motivating factors identified during discovery.
- Collaborate with other project team members regularly to ensure that the communication plan timing aligns nicely with other milestones.
- Establish a centralized and transparent repository for questions, ideas, and comments from change community members.
- Establish a regular meeting cadence with project and communication stakeholders to draft, review, edit, approve, and track executed messaging.
- Initiate and establish a regular meeting cadence with community representatives (champions) to validate discovery, facilitate timely communication, ensure relevance, identify FAQs and motivating factors, and build rapport.

Design, Develop and Deliver Training and Provide Support

- Develop a detailed plan for instructional development and the completion of related deliverables, incorporate preferences identified during discovery, and execute.
- Finalize the training plan and calendar ideally 6 weeks prior to training to allow community members to plan. Send invitations when confident that you will meet the date, with project and communication activities. Agree on a training go-no/go date with your project team colleagues.
- Complete one or more training pilots, evaluate and incorporate feedback to improve, and align with testing whenever possible.
- Execute training as indicated on the training plan.
- Establish a plan for how to get help, post training, and incorporate reminders in communication plan messaging.
- Facilitate post-training support until inquiries dwindle.

Ensure Technology and Process Alignment—Testing for Effectiveness on a Small Group

- Align instructional development and training pilot efforts with user acceptance testing efforts whenever possible if the change involves technology implementation.
- Enlist representatives of the community to complete user acceptance testing using relevant business scenarios (if there is a technology component) or provide reactions

APPENDIX PROCESS AND TOOLS

- or feedback on proposed activities/content/tools for nontechnical changes.
- Evaluate for simplicity, user reaction, reception, opportunity to remove barriers, opportunity to improve usability, and alignment with visionary goals and objectives.
- Allow time to incorporate user and community member feedback to ensure a positive first impression upon introduction.

Promote Transparent Accountability and Provide Recognition

- Establish key performance indicators from which to establish accountability and measure success as early as you can. Determine how to capture, publish, and align with measurable objectives identified during discovery.
- Begin to measure key performance indicators and results as soon as you are able.
- Publish measurements to the entire community and work with senior-most leaders to deliver initial post-rollout messaging to recognize achievement and establish accountability.
- Establish an ongoing cadence for reporting results and incorporate into a communication plan to ensure ongoing recognition and accountability until habits are developed.
- Provide coaching to senior-most leaders on how to evaluate results using tools and provide timely recognition and communication.

Iterate and Improve

- Identify areas to target and address them with appropriate interventions, continue measurement to evaluate effectiveness and improvement.
- Solicit ideas and feedback and establish a process for receipt and response.
- Define the process for ongoing governance and establish ownership for continuity.
- 'Facilitate knowledge transfer to transition from the initial change cycle to a subsequent change cycle or ongoing governance.
- Initiate the cadence for ongoing governance to ensure continuity.
- Articulate new objectives and establish the vision for subsequent change cycle(s).
- Allow measurements to evolve and mature as new discoveries are made.

APPENDIX PROCESS AND TOOLS

If you plug these sample activities into a spreadsheet with completion milestones across a series of months, you end up with a simplified Gantt view of milestones that looks something like this:

CHANGE MANAGEMENT ACTIVITY	Dec	Jan	Feb	Mar	Apr	May	Jun	Jul	Aug	Sep	Oct	Nov	Dec
Project Kickoff	■												
Visionary Messaging Complete and Executed		■											
Discovery Complete			■										
Initial Draft of Project and Communication Plan				■									
Curriculum Map Complete						■							
Training Plan/ Schedule Established									■				
Support Plan Established								■					
Training Development Complete											■		
User Acceptance Testing Complete (if applicable)											■		
Systems of Accountability and Feedback Established											■		
Continuity/ Governance Plan in Place												■	
Objectives and Vision Defined for Next Change Cycle													■

You can see the blown-out version of an example of a full change management plan with even more detailed activities on the Symphony website (thesymphonymethod.com). There we'll also provide a recommendation of how to align sprints with change management cycles for organizations using Agile project methodologies.

CHANGE MANAGEMENT DELIVERABLES

When I embark on a project, I typically outline the deliverables that my customers can expect to see throughout the life of a project. I'm going to provide you with the definition and purpose of the superset list of change management deliverables but will direct you to my website (thesymphonymethod.com) for actual examples.

1. **Meeting Agendas and Summaries**: These may seem like obvious no-brainers, but one of the ways we build trust and rapport, gain credibility, and reach agreement is by establishing plans for our interactions and summarizing our understanding of what we hear. Meeting summaries also provide an opportunity for people to add to, improve, or correct understanding. This practice also helps people who are unable to participate in certain interactions to stay informed. Through the early discovery processes we meet with many people and learn so much. Often the only way to keep track of it all is to proactively set the stage for our meetings, take thorough notes, send meeting summaries to participants, and post them in a centralized and transparent spot so we can refer back to any decision points.

APPENDIX PROCESS AND TOOLS

2. **Change Management Summary:** This document is a one-time document published following discovery that outlines the overall intended change management approach. Its sections define the roles of the change community members, the numbers of people who fall into each role, the objectives and desired outcomes of the projects, the best methods for reaching change communities through regular communication, the recommended instructional deliverables and training delivery methods, the recommended metrics for building accountability, and the approach for ensuring continuity. This document shouldn't contain anything that you can't back up with notes or meeting summaries in your discovery sessions.

   I typically circulate this document with key leaders and project stakeholders and hold a meeting to review and request approval and agreement for the go-forward approach. Once that agreement is achieved, we can move from discovery to execution, and refer back to the Change Management Summary to communicate the planned approach as new stakeholders, such as champion representatives, join the effort.

3. **Change Management and Communication Plan:** The change management and communication plan is the waterfall-esque project plan that helps us proactively plan our communication and all other change management activities, week-by-week throughout the initial change

cycle. This is a working document that will continue to evolve throughout the project, just like any project plan. I typically start with a milestone Gantt like the one shown earlier in this chapter and then build the more granular activities around those milestones until I have a workable project plan. If the change management initiative is to be aligned with a technical solution, these milestones need to be embedded and aligned with the technology project plan.

If you're aligning your change management and communication plans with Agile methodology, you'll participate in backlog refinement sessions to determine which of the instructional and communication elements will be reflected in a particular epic or sprint. I will say, however, that some change management tasks require long-term, proactive planning because members of our change communities, sometimes in large numbers, have to plan their lives around them. The practice of meeting change deadlines also lends credibility to the team, the leadership, and the initiative. Projects rely on budget, scope, and time. Agile provides flexibility and focus. I found a nice balance using a hybrid approach, especially for the first change cycle, that one of my colleagues once referred to as *Wagile*. I also find that while the initial change management cycle used for an initial implementation benefits from some waterfall style elements, subsequent iterative cycles like those we experience when managing ongoing governance often settle in nicely to a more purely Agile approach.

4. **Messaging:** The plan tells us *when* we're communicating, and the messaging is *what* we're communicating. Imagine a word document, email draft or PowerPoint presentation for each one of the messages you have on your plan. Messaging can be delivered using a variety of delivery methods at a timing that often begins with less frequent delivery and increases in frequency the closer we come to an actual go-live date. The deliverable by the person managing the change is often a content outline, or a drafted message that helps the deliverers of the message know what to say and is fine tuned through an editing and approval process before execution.

A Word of Caution: The worst kind of communication is that which never occurs. Overthinking and overanalyzing content can lead to delays that result in irrelevance or even completely missed opportunities. Multiple rounds of edits, in most cases, don't lend significantly to the quality of the messaging. This is a great example of where good is important, but perfect is often not. Have a little fun with this—no need to make it harder than it has to be.

Oh! And one more thing...just like everything else, people have very different preferences for how they like to be communicated with. Some people don't want to have too much detail, and some people want to have access to every detail. I find providing both is really easy to do. You can include a quick, executive-style bulleted summary in an email and include a more detailed leadership brief or project update in an attachment, so your change community gets the best of both worlds.

The idea is to serve the most common preferences of the entire user community and help people feel they are well informed. Your preferences, related to what level of detail makes *you* feel informed, are very likely not the same as everyone else's.

5. **Frequently Asked Questions (FAQ):** The FAQ list is often linked to the messages we send that are tracked on our Change Management and Communication Plan. It is initiated at the very beginning of the project, even when we're getting questions from our earliest stakeholders. This is a working document that is maintained by change managers but will undoubtedly require input from business and IT leaders and stakeholders. It evolves over time, starting with questions about the vision and what we're trying to accomplish, and moving on to questions about progress, training, getting help, metrics and, finally, about what's next. I like to keep the answers in a centralized spot, like a SharePoint or Google document that people can easily access and bookmark. It makes it easy to transparently acknowledge and answer questions as they come in. An FAQ is one of the tools we use to build transparency and rapport with the larger change community.
6. **Curriculum Map:** This document is the first deliverable of an instructional development effort. It articulates who the different learners are, what we want them to know how to

do in the form of instructional objectives, what business scenarios we might use to help make the learning concept most relevant, and what delivery methods we plan to use for training. Instructional developers use this tool as an outline from which they build instructional deliverables. The curriculum map is the product of the analysis and design phases of the ADDIE instructional systems design model. I referred to this tool during the capability section, so I won't review it again here, but I do provide a sample curriculum map on the Symphony website (thesymphonymethod.com) for your perusal.

7. **Training Plan:** While instructional development occurs, change managers or training project resources will begin planning the execution or delivery of training. Training plans vary by delivery method. For example, a live or virtual class will have a specific date, start time, end time, duration, and possibly a maximum capacity. This kind of session requires assigning participants to classes or a sign-up process to provide options. The end result is a calendar, a sign-up process, and spreadsheet detailing the dates, times, participants, and location information (or virtual conference information) for the class. For self-paced delivery methods, teams will often post the e-learning or video modules in a Learning Management System (LMS) where they can track learner completion.

For technology projects, sometimes teams need to establish training environments, training logins, and business scenarios with relevant data that support the learning objectives. Those logistics should also be detailed in the various training plan worksheets.

The training plan can be initiated quite early in the change management process because through discovery, you'll determine the approach and can start arranging logistics and details. Like the change management and communication plans, it becomes a working document since you'll continue to finalize and fill in the details throughout the project. I use multi-worksheet spreadsheets for my training plans, and in particularly complex projects may use a separate spreadsheet for tracking class registration and participation.

Finally, especially for technology projects, work with your technology team and project manager to establish a "ready-to-schedule training" milestone. The purpose of this milestone is to gain agreement from all other project stakeholders that they have the confidence that the system is tracking to be ready around the time of training, and that it is okay to send save-the-date or actual invitations with details. Even if you don't know all of the detailed training dates, it is respectful to give your learners a heads up many weeks in advance so they can plan their personal and business lives around upcoming training expectations. Ideally, we want to send the training schedule out only one time, because pushing dates detracts from team credibility and perceived success. The ready-to-schedule training milestone helps us to minimize the likelihood of pushing dates.

8. **Test Plan Scenarios:** While I don't necessarily think it is the role of the change manager and/or instructional developer to develop test plans for all user stories or requirements, I do think creating an alliance between those responsible for quality assurance, user acceptance testing, and the change management team is incredibly helpful for ensuring a positive user acceptance testing experience and first impression of the system. Instructional Developers work with subject matter experts to come up with use cases or user scenarios that make the learning relevant. If we can incorporate those same relevant user scenarios in the test plans, we typically have more relevant test cases and can use the testing experience to build proficiency among the representatives of our community even faster. If you're developing work instructions or a step-by-step user manual, a designated person should follow those instructions as a test to ensure the quality and accuracy of the detailed instructions. Using the UAT orientation as an opportunity to pilot the flow of the training can also lend to the thoroughness of the testing. The **UAT milestone** is another handshake milestone that should be aligned with any technical project plans, as it is critical to bringing together the curriculum development, training communication, and technology first-impression elements of the change initiative.

9. **Training Deliverables:** As I mentioned in the Building Capability chapter, there are several possible instructional deliverables. Here's a list of what an instructional developer might deliver.

a. Documented step-by-step instructions (Playbook, User Guide)

b. Participant workbooks (relevant reading and hands-on scenarios or activities that support learning objectives)

c. PowerPoint presentations (to guide the flow of learning in class, on screen or in a train-the-trainer environment)

d. Self-paced learning modules (built in Camtasia, Captivate, Adobe Connect, Articulate, or other learning development solutions)

e. Micro-learning videos (short subject videos used to complement or reinforce learning objectives, ideally 6–10 minutes in length, produced as MP4s, and uploadable to a variety of different learning platforms including many LMS tools, YouTube, Vimeo, and Salesforce's MyTrailhead)

f. Leader's notes (prompts for instructors who might be in a position to teach the developed course, typically distributed prior to a train-the-trainer event)

10. **Support Plan:** Whether provided through change management communication or through the technology project team, the change community needs to know how to get help as issues or questions arise. This is often a

APPENDIX PROCESS AND TOOLS

simple one-page document sent through a message that explains a support hierarchy. Level 1 might be self-help (like consulting your user documentation), level 2 could be asking your champion, level 3 could escalate to the project team, level 4 could escalate to an IT or steering committee team, and level 5 may even include escalating to technology or concept vendors. Levels 3 and beyond may require the community member to submit an inquiry or question using an online form that either creates a case or adds to a spreadsheet monitored by the team. The support plan is a simple, one-page document that is an important part of the overall plan and fosters ongoing rapport with the change community.

11. **Documented Measurements to Drive Accountability:** This is not so much a delivered document as it is ensuring the metrics are captured, evaluated, communicated, and recognized. Much of my recent work has been supporting different application implementations using the Salesforce platform. Salesforce has a straightforward capability for building reports and reflecting key measurements on a dashboard, including the ability to capture a snapshot in time so you can report on trends. Forwarding these links, or even capturing a screenshot once a week to keep the progress measurements top-of-mind is easy to do by incorporating them into the regular communication cadence. Regardless of the change initiative, however, regular measurements need to be captured and evaluated in comparison to prior progress or a benchmark to show progress, stagnation, or a slide in the wrong direction.

Measurements help us to understand where we need to target our efforts and what we can celebrate. For this deliverable, envision reports, dashboards, or even spreadsheets that allow us to chart our success, and share it on a regular basis to our change community.

12. **Continuity Plan:** This is the newest deliverable for me, but it is critical to the ongoing iteration and ultimate engagement of the change. The purpose of this document is to state how the key stakeholders of the project will work together to ensure that the change initiative continues to evolve and progress, and that ideas are considered, prioritized, and put into action if the decisions are made to do so. Think of the continuity plan as a set of bylaws.

    Here are some examples of what might be included in a continuity plan document:

    a. Definition of the cadence for ongoing meetings and communication activities, the role responsible for organizing, and the expected participants of a governing or steering committee.

    b. List of named champions, and a plan for refreshing the role at six- or twelve-month intervals.

    c. A how-to document for submitting an idea or request to the team responsible for prioritization.

    d. A simple, written outline of the ongoing governance

APPENDIX PROCESS AND TOOLS

decision-making process and related definitions.

e. Links to a site for ongoing access to training and support, monitored by a governance steering committee or center of excellence.

f. An archive of past project deliverables and knowledge transfer documents that can be used as templates or reference for future projects.

g. Definitions of systems used for receiving, storing, and evaluating ideas for improvements.

h. Definition of elements for subsequent change cycles.

i. Definition of objectives identified during the first change cycle that should be considered for a subsequent change cycle. (This can be used to seed the effort.)

The continuity plan will definitely differ depending on the type of change initiative, but a good final deliverable for an initial change cycle is to support the definition, formation, and initial activities of the continuity, governance, or ongoing steering committee.

So...that wraps up the appendix. Riveting, right? I know it was for at least a few! The purpose of this chapter was to give you some tools you can use to support your change initiative at each step of the way. If you'd like to see some examples, please take a look at the Symphony website (thesymphonymethod.com). I hope the visualization is useful in helping you bring your upcoming change initiatives to fruition.

PIONEERS OF PROFESSIONAL DEVELOPMENT, PROCESS IMPROVEMENT, AND CHANGE MANAGEMENT

THIS BOOK IS A HOW-TO GUIDE for managing change for leaders. My intent has been to provide a comprehensive, step-by-step approach to managing change so that even when budgets run out and organizations decide to manage change using people who are doing this in addition to their "day jobs," they have a resource that provides one way of doing it well.

I can't finish a how-to guide for managing change without giving credit to some of the pioneers of change management who framed my education and experience in this area and listing some resources that might be helpful for you should you decide to continue your own self-education on the subject.

MAGER AND PIPE

The authors who have had the most influence on my work to date are Robert Mager and Peter Pipe, who were recommended to me by a very talented instructional systems design mentor. These two authors developed a performance analysis model way back in 1970 that they built into a book series called the *Mager Six Pack*, initially published in 1984. That *Mager Six Pack* has helped me to learn how to write effective, performance-based instruction. I referred to the work of these gentlemen early in this book when I introduced their diagnostic approach to non-performance, which was included in another of their books, *What Every Manager Should Know About Training*.

One of the things that was so enlightening about these books when I first read them in the 1990s was that as leaders, we tend to *assume* that if someone isn't performing in a certain way, it probably means that they don't know how. So we send people through training again (which is often expensive) and sometimes are surprised when training doesn't solve the problem. If we were to take the time to evaluate why the person isn't meeting expectations consistently, we might find that there are other reasons (often with much more effective and less expensive remedies than training) that people don't perform in the way we want them to.

The greatest impact the Mager and Pipe Performance Analysis model has had on my change management work is the diagnostic flowchart used to determine why individual contributors might not perform. When applied from a leadership perspective, a manager might identify an individual who is not meeting the objectives as required, and this diagnostic tool takes the manager through a flowchart with a series of questions and suggestions that help that person get back on track.

How is this relevant to managing change? Because managing change is simply applying a proactive approach to moving *many* individuals to perform in a desired way. Organizations are made up of a whole bunch of individuals. If we can proactively anticipate why people might not change and do our best to address all those reasons in advance, we have a recipe for success.

This recipe works for small teams, medium teams, and even huge teams because we simply anticipate why an individual contributor may or may not be prepared to perform in a way that we want them to, and proactively address those reasons to minimize non-performance.

It also turns out that applying performance models proactively helps us to empathize, communicate effectively, proactively prepare, and more authentically interact with our teams. In essence, it helps us to do the things that organizations with excellent cultures do. Quite a bonus!

The excellent work of Mager and Pipe laid the foundation for the instructional development work I've been doing for decades. If you're in training and development and haven't had the pleasure of reading these books yet, I highly recommend them. Their work is so timeless that they still get 4.5–5-star reviews after all these years.

THE TIPPING POINT

This is another must read for leaders in all roles who are influencing change. *The Tipping Point* by Malcolm Gladwell examines the bell curve of change and how to strategically employ influential people to help you drive the change. When we're working with large groups of people, we tend to focus a whole lot of energy on the few people who don't want to change rather than focusing our energy on the majority of people.

The Tipping Point refers to that point, like the over-the-top point on a roller coaster, when momentum takes over. Sometimes you have to really work to get to the top of that hill, and it feels like you're having to pull people up or push from behind. There is a point, though, when the majority of people get on board. This is when the momentum takes over, and the change you wish to see simply becomes "the way things are done." This book discusses strategies for achieving this tipping point. Thank You, Mr. Gladwell, for a great read!

The Tipping Point also serves as a gentle reminder (for me, anyway) that there will always be a few people who are simply *not* going to willingly get there. If we spend the majority of our time, energy, and resources working on getting those few people to adopt a change, then we're doing a significant disservice to the majority of the people who *will* get there willingly. Also—once you've reached the tipping point and momentum takes over, the few people who are dragging their feet generally get pulled along.

DALE CARNEGIE

When I was fifteen years old, I won a scholarship to attend a Dale Carnegie course in Human Relations and Effective Speaking. I remember being in a room full of established professional people feeling pretty uncomfortable, and I felt even more uncomfortable when I had to speak in front of them. I completed the course, though. I had no idea how important that introduction was to my career.

If communicating, facilitating, talking, or writing is scary for you, invest the time to practice these skills. They are at the core of every influential leader, and Mr. Carnegie's timeless concepts are every bit as relevant today as they ever were. For some, authentic communication seems to come naturally, but I believe that most great communicators have a great deal of study and practice behind them. These skills can definitely be learned, and like all skills, they get better with practice.

Authentic communication, relating to people, communicating effectively, and establishing rapport are all at the forefront of managing change. Using a repeatable process ensures that people know what we want them to do, and why we want them to do it. We proactively anticipate the factors that motivate people and how we're going to teach them. If we're good, we also have measurable goals and systems of accountability in place. But at the center of it all is authentic communication and connection. Dale Carnegie was a master! I know the Dale Carnegie organization is still alive and well today, and *How to Win Friends and Influence People* (written in 1936) is one of the best-selling books of all time.

SIX SIGMA AND LEAN MANUFACTURING PRINCIPLES

One of the other organizations that has been quite influential in my methodology for managing change Is Lean Six Sigma. I gained Six Sigma's Green Belt credential in the early 2000s, and the concepts helped me to see change management as a cycle (when done well) instead of a linear, one-time event.

At the core of Six Sigma is DMAIC (Define, Measure, Analyze, Improve, Control), its methodology for improving a particular process.

In the Six Sigma coursework, one measures success in the form of defects per million. It encourages a cyclic approach to applying and reapplying this DMAIC method to move you closer to your Six Sigma goal of 3.14 defects per million parts, which is a pretty great quality rate.

The Six Sigma program is a process improvement/quality management approach that can be applied to the process of managing organizational change. We define what we want to have happen, we determine how we're going to measure it, we analyze all the factors that are going to influence the adoption of the change, and we act on those insights or improve.

For me, the most influential aspect was learning that once we've implemented the first set of improvements, we measure again, analyze our results, determine how to improve again, and continue the cycle until we've reached an acceptable result. Once we've reached that goal, we incorporate some ongoing metrics into our performance-measurement dashboards to help us to control or maintain our good results.

Thank you to the Lean Six Sigma program and to the Japanese manufacturing process improvement concepts that influenced it for helping my change management methodology become an iterative cycle.

IN CLOSING

My approach to managing change has evolved with years of practice and life experience and has become common sense to me. I have been honing these skills for twenty-five years, and I feel like now is an excellent time to put them into a how-to book. Right now, we need caring, service-minded leaders who are skilled in the art of intentionally guiding the changes that are occurring in their organizations and in the world, and this book introduces one way to do it, drawing on concepts that may already feel familiar to you.

Thank you for reading this book and considering my approach, and I hope you'll consider some of these resources as you mature in your own capability. I wish you the best of success with your change endeavors and invite you to share your comments and your own recommendations as we continue the collaboration as a change management community.

ACKNOWLEDGMENTS

TO TERRY NORSTRUD, thank you for seeing my potential and encouraging me to pursue it. May you feel my gratitude as you rest peacefully.

To Sylvia Poage, thank you for introducing me to Mager and Pipe, and for taking the time to give me an abundance of thoughtful redlines that led to a high standard of excellence, interesting work, and a fun career.

To Bruce Kawahara, thank you for your early coaching and mentorship. You introduced me to the concept of an organization's personality, the ability to feel its ease or angst, and you proved that with intentional work, a struggling culture can be changed.

To Eric Berridge, thank you for modeling what it means to be a service-minded leader, and for regularly asking, "How can I help?" The combination of your intentional vision, the amazing people we worked with, the standards to which we held ourselves accountable, and the impactful work we did resulted in the best of cultures.

To Amy Collette, thank you for guiding me on this journey to become an author, for your gentle prodding, and for your thoughtful contributions. Mission Accomplished!

ABOUT THE AUTHOR

Photograph by Stephen Russell

TRICIA BENNETT has a passion for leadership, talent management, and employee engagement, but most importantly, she is an advocate for people. A service-minded leader, Tricia knows that if you provide the people you serve with a clear vision, kindness and respect, they will work alongside you to achieve that vision in a way that exceeds your expectations and builds a culture of excellence and loyalty.

An organizational change management leader, Tricia has been a consultant for nearly 20 years, leading teams to implement solutions built on the Salesforce platform. She has both experienced and influenced the cultures of numerous organizations which have contributed to her beliefs and to her Symphony Method for managing change.

Tricia is also a registered nurse, a credential she gained later in her career. Working as a nurse expanded her compassion for the human experience, her understanding of how truly unique each person is, and how important it is to ask for people's perspectives rather than to assume them. TheSymphonyMethod.com

Made in the USA
Columbia, SC
09 February 2022